An Extra Year

Grief and Loss in the New Age

ISBN: 1-4392-0757-7
ISBN-13: 9781439207574

Visit www.booksurge.com to order additional copies.

For all of us

The minute I heard my first love story

I started looking for you, not knowing

how blind that was.

Lovers don't finally meet somewhere.

They're in each other all along.

-Rumi

(Translated by Coleman Barks)

Table of Contents

Introduction

My partner died. Or "died." The quotes are because my take on what died means is not entirely conventional, yet it's hardly novel either. It just doesn't seem like the most accurate description of what happens, at least not when we take into consideration the *being* part of human being. And when he crossed over or made his transition or departed this plane (you get the idea), I entered what is commonly referred to in our culture as a process of grief and loss. Or "grief and loss." These quotes are because my own personal journey along this most universal path was also, apparently, not entirely conventional either.

And that's really all this book is about – one man's process (and it is, indeed, a process) of adjusting to life without his life partner. I have no doubt you will navigate through it quite easily but there are a few things that will help. First, I refer to him as my partner because when we met, it was just one of those things. Just one of those crazy…I'm kidding, I'm not going to make you sing that song but you do need to know it was really one of those cosmic, wham, hello there, wow, and yes, yes, yes things. We used the term "partner" from the beginning because we felt like partners. Egalitarian. Teammates. I experienced it as twin energy or what I imagined twin energy might feel like. The point is we were going to be together and we knew it and that was that.

Another thing is his name was Steve and everybody who knew him, knew him as Steve. That was my name, too, until I went to college and started going by Steven. But when he talked about me he called me Steve and when we met new people together anything could happen but almost always we were Steven & Steve or Steve & Steve. And all of this is to say that with all the Stevens and Steves flying around us all the time, we never called each other either one. Ever. (Unless we were trying to crack the other one up, but that's another story.) Rather, two men with the same name, in love and embarking on the relationship they thought from the start would be *the* relationship, lasting decades, wound up with the same nickname for each other: Duder. Don't even ask. It just came up one day soon after we met and stuck – like the craziest of glues – such that we virtually never addressed the other one without using it. *Hey Duder, what do you think about this? Well, Duder, I think this and that. Yeah, me too, Duder. Thanks, Duder. Do you think we say 'Duder' enough? Ha, ha, ha.*

Living it was natural but writing it is fairly embarrassing and I'd have happily left this part out but I had to tell you because it's what I call him in this book. I tried to write it using his actual name, which I typically use when I talk about him to others. But when I attempted to do that here, in writing, for months, it felt as though I was talking about someone else and the disconnection smothered the process. So he was formally known in this world as Steven Michael Lewis and informally as Steve Lewis. But he was known in my world – and now yours – as Duder.

(Not to belabor the point but this is particularly amusing because when he was here and people would hang out with us, it didn't take long for them to pick up on the Duder thing and start calling us by our nicknames. I always thought it was endearing but Duder? Not so much. In fact, he absolutely forbid it. "Duder" was just for him and me and it stayed that way. Until now.)

Finally, something about my work. Essentially, it's about helping people live spiritually responsible lives and at its core are 15 concepts, all of which are universally spiritual and none of which I made up. I simply culled them from the overabundance of teachings available to us at the dawn of a new age and then got really good at seeing – and eventually helping others to see – how and where they show up in our daily lives. That's what I do (an evolution of having been a psychotherapist) and I mention it only because the concepts form a lens through which I tend to see the world and so they appear throughout the book. When they come up, I put them in italics and they are:

Be compassionate • Beliefs matter • Be present
Choices abound • Everything is energy
Have an attitude of gratitude • Intentions matter
Judgments separate us
Listen to inspiration • Mind and body are connected
Take responsibility
The law of attraction governs us all • We are all connected
We are here for a reason
We belong to the planet, not the planet to us

∞

This is my story. I lived it through and through, embodied it, and I've been told it's a very personal one. But it doesn't feel that way to me. Somewhere along the line it became clear that it was no longer for me, for just me. My *intention* for sharing it with you – and, if I may, mine and Duder's *intention* – is that it may offer some degree of healing, some uplift for you and anyone you know who may be in the grips of healing a loss experience.

It is truly an honor to meet you in this place of discovery and unfolding at this moment in time when old paradigms are falling by the wayside and new ones are emerging in their places. As we learn and create new ways to teach our children, to take care of our bodies, to be in relationship, to do business, to care for the planet, and infinitely more, so, too, are we discovering more and more about our spiritual side, the being part of us, and new paradigms, even, for "grief and loss."

P E A C E .

Steven Morrison
Idyllwild, CA
June, 2008

"You'll Know"

December 21, 2005

The time for some much-needed alone time had finally arrived and I was grateful beyond measure. It was nearly sunset on December 21 which, in southern California, comes startlingly early — somewhere around 4:30 in the afternoon. Watching the sun set just beyond the horizon of the Pacific had long ago become a staple of beach living for me and sharing it with Duder for the the last two years had turned it into something exponentially exceptional. Sometimes it would be elaborately planned with appetizers, ice-cold beers, and the intimacy of two people in love and loving being together. Other times it would catch us off-guard and we'd rush home to enjoy as much of it as we could. Once in a while we'd walk the block and a half to the beach and watch it with bare feet in the sand. And sometimes, like tonight, I'd enjoy it all by myself.

Freshly-lit candles added some magic to the feeling in the house and I was taken aback when I realized I had lit them. In fact, I'd been organizing myself for the evening event utterly free of conscious thought. A peek in the fridge, but not really in the mood for any of that; a mix of soft music, for some reason, in favor of the absolute silence I typically prefer; a check of the clouds — always a strong indicator of the type of sunset to come and on this night foretelling a spectacular show; an adjustment of the sliding screen door to the other side for a view through clear glass; and, finally, a comfortable perch on the couch because this one would be enjoyed from inside given the cold air and really strong breezes outside.

Settling in and breathing a very deep sigh, I was mesmerized by the various versions of yellows and reds and blues and pinks undulating through the clouds. I could feel the richness of the sky as I continued breathing deeply, watching the brilliance of Mother Nature doing her Mother Nature thing, and thinking about how fitting it was that this particularly gorgeous sunset would occur on the winter solstice. And as is my sunset custom, I offered a note of gratitude to All That Is for the sunset itself and the goings-on of the day, and felt the humility that comes with being able to enjoy such a life of privilege. I got up off the couch and took a few steps to the glass where I could take in even more of the sky's magnificence. My gaze was unbroken, my body was still, my thoughts were a blur and wham! There he was. In my chest! Filling it and then some. In a nanosecond I felt a tsunami of love come over and through and into me that was so pure and so powerful and so unmistakably him, so unmistakably us. He was right: I knew. It had only been 19 hours since he left his body and 16 hours since it was carried out of the house by the Keystone Cops of undertakers, wrapped in a sheet, and taken to a mortuary 15 miles away. But oh how he was here. With me. In the house. In *my* body. During the sunset. No doubt about it. And what transpired was something I'd never experienced before – or since.

I stayed right where I was, still gazing at the luminous and hypnotic sky, feeling him and feeling our own specific brand of love. Then all at once I started to know things. The first thing I knew was that he was with his brother, Ron, who had made his transition 14 years earlier. We had talked extensively of his being reunited with this soul whom he loved so much and it was comforting to know that something we thought might occur, something I had thought would offer him great comfort in his transition, was actually happening. Already! He was telling me, as their reunion was underway, that his spiritual partnership with his brother spanned myriad lifetimes, was of tremendous proportions, and was built upon great mutual love, admiration, and respect. And he was telling me that our spiritual partnership also spanned myriad lifetimes, was of tremendous proportions, and was built upon great mutual love, admiration, and respect. And despite these identical descriptions, he let me know that the two relationships were entirely different from one another. I also knew as I continued to look at the ever-changing colors of the sky that he was well, doing well, and happy. He was happy! We also chuckled, however it is that beings chuckle when having spontaneous inter-dimensional telepathic conversations, about how we were sharing another sunset together, albeit somewhat differently. Okay, completely differently. I was blown away.

I'd say my attention drifted but it feels more accurate to say it was placed – on a song that had begun to play on the stereo. It was part of a mix of music that we'd had going for a few weeks and this particular song was a favorite of mine, which I think he knew. What he didn't know is that whenever I heard it, I privately dedicated it to God and offered it as a prayer of sorts. The song is *Kind and Generous,* by Natalie Merchant, and I was about to shift my habit and dedicate it to him but something rather forceful stopped me and said, listen. Just listen. ...*For your kindness, I'm in debt to you; for your selflessness, my admiration; for everything you've done, you know I'm bound to thank you for it*...It was him expressing his thanks to me for taking care of him – via that song – in a way he never had when he was so ill and preparing to leave this plane. Not that he had to, I knew he was grateful. But this was different. He had a strength now that had been lost during his last months and weeks of life here and an ability, apparently, to shut me up. He made me listen and he made me know those words were from him to me...*and I never could have come this far without you*...*I want to thank you for so many gifts you gave with love and tenderness*...*I want to thank you for your generosity, the love and the honesty that you gave me*...*I want to thank you, show my gratitude, my love and my respect for you*...And with this act he reminded me of how deliciously humbling it feels to be on the receiving end of pure appreciation. And why I'd put on the music.

So there was what I knew from what he was telling me and there was what I felt. My experience was that this encounter was decidedly un-rushed with plenty of time – 20 minutes? 40 minutes? – to feel emotions ranging from love to glee to humility to sorrow to appreciation to joy to wonder to longing to peace and then some. And like a pinball in a game with no control over its own destiny, I went up to, back from, and across again to each of those emotions over and over in a rapid yet lovingly gentle manner, as if I and everything I "hit" were wrapped in cotton. Not only did I feel so full of so much feeling, I felt the feeling in ways I never had before. I felt it in my body – permeating my veins, arteries, and capillaries; my organs, muscles, and bones – and I felt it all as it anchored itself in my cells.

Perhaps you think me a bit off my rocker. A crystal clear, telepathic conversation with my very recently departed partner? Yeah right. Probably just the result of an overactive imagination about to be deluged by waves of grief and loss. I had moments of second-guessing it all myself, believe me, but what lured me back from second-guessing, what was unmistakable and impossible to ignore, was the utterly unrestrained feeling I had afterward. I felt as though my soul had grown, as if it had been promoted somehow, and that I was suddenly a more expanded version of myself. Still me, for sure, but bigger – on the inside. And part of what I knew right then, in the aftermath of this telephathic conversation I'd just had with my "dead" partner and as I continued to gaze at the now darkening sky, was that I would go forth in my life a stronger, more confident, better version of myself; that my two "short" years with him and the experience of helping him to leave when it was the last thing I wanted to do, was a seminal point in my own growth and development and one which I could clearly see would not have been realized had he stayed.

∞

While telepathic conversation was brand new to my experience, communication with the other side was anything but. In 1998, when I was fully engaged in seeking all things spiritual and after I had wholeheartedly embraced the concept of life on the other side of the veil, Elizabeth entered my life. Right on schedule. She is a clairvoyant (clear seeing) and I, eager at the time to learn about and meet any and all spirit guides I may have had (because I'd just learned about the concept of them), jumped at the opportunity to schedule my first reading with her. She has since become a very close friend and will tell you that from day one I said I wanted to be able to communicate with the other side on my own.

The way it works in session with Elizabeth — and this will be quite helpful for you to know — is that you and she are seated comfortably in chairs and with seemingly minimal preparation on her part, the show begins. By that I mean she tunes in to a frequency whereby she can see non-physical beings and receive communication from them telepathically and through pictures — moving and still, apparently — which they show her like some inter-dimensional game of charades. On occasion I've also known her to hear them (clairaudience), but mostly it's pictures and telepathy. And as far as I'm concerned, there are a few things that set her apart from others who do what she does. One of them is that she is gifted in her ability to describe in great detail not only the beings she sees — what they look like, how big or small they are, how they may be dressed, where they may be in the room, etc. — but also what they show her with their still and moving pictures. She also possesses a fearlessness about what she may be shown at any given moment, which means she is shown a very wide range of material. And she's not at all woo-woo which, combined with a reverent dose of irreverence, makes for some entertaining exchanges. Ultimately, a reading with Elizabeth is like using an interpreter to talk with someone who speaks a different language and she's the interpreter. In my years of experience with her, I will say unequivocally that communication on the whole is extremely clear. My first time, however, it took a little while.

Two beings appeared in that first reading as an old couple and Elizabeth's descriptions of them were not recognizable to me at all. They seemed to be saying that they were grandparents or perhaps great-grandparents, but that didn't resonate either because three of my grandparents had crossed over well before I was born and the fourth, my mother's mother, had made her transition before I was two. So I never knew my grandparents, but I had often wondered if any of them were "watching over" me. From this exchange, I assumed they weren't because what I knew of them from stories and pictures was not reflected in anything Elizabeth was saying. And if they were great-grandparents, I'd really have no way of knowing that. So we let it slide and went on with the session because sometimes, I later learned, it just goes that way.

More conversation ensued about things I couldn't connect with and even though I'd gone in with no skepticism at all, I was now beginning to wonder. Where was the glitz? The fun? The awe? Then the couple talked about an incident that happened when I was 14 or 15. I was having a particularly rough time when my overpowering rage drove me to the brink. After screaming myself hoarse and throwing and breaking things with a force I didn't know I had and dramatically stomping up the 15 stairs to my room, slamming the door sending the jam flying and feeling like I hadn't come close to exhausting all I had inside of me, I sat on my bed, eyes shut tight, shaking, certain that if I continued for one more minute I would go completely insane and that if I stopped I wouldn't. It was that simple. Consciously *choosing* sanity as a teenager was a momentous act which I didn't/couldn't share with anyone. More than 20 years later, these beings were telling me that they were there then, sitting with me on the bed, helping me to make that choice. Bye bye skepticism.

I scheduled another reading and in the days leading up to it began to think about my friend, Richard, who had crossed over two or three years earlier and with whom I'd had a particular piece of unfinished business. So I went into session two with a question for Elizabeth: Could I "dial up" specific people I knew who had crossed over and talk with them? Her answer was, "Who's Richard?" He was right there and I knew it because her description of him was right on the money. We chatted for a bit, he and I, laughed some, and finished the unfinished business. My sense of the non-physical world was expanding at warp speed.

At the time, I had been reading lots of modern spirituality books and had soaked up all they had to say before realizing that, to a large degree, they were saying very similar things. So I was looking for something new to challenge and advance my growth and it occurred to me that weekly sessions with Elizabeth and the non-physicals would be far more productive than therapy or anything else I could think of. And that's what I did for about a year and a half. The older couple didn't return, but in their place came a bevy of non-physical guides and angels and teachers – something like 12 to 15 of them! I'd seen plenty of books about meeting your spirit guide or your guardian angel. Were they kidding? I had a ton of them and my greatest desire was to learn to communicate with them without Elizabeth.

Somewhere along the line I had picked up the *belief* that feeling the tingly body thing we all feel – "goosebumps" and "chills" – was a little hello of sorts from the other side. As my readings with Elizabeth progressed, I noticed more and more tingly body sensations and was convinced that different sensations – heavier and lighter, this part of the body vs. that part – were associated with the different non-physicals who were working with me at the time. I got mildly obsessed not only with attempting to decipher who it was at any given moment that was "sending tinglies" but also what it was they were trying to communicate by doing so. And was that even how it worked? Did they really "send" them? Did they really "direct" them to certain parts of the body? Were they trying to tell me something? Was there a particular reason I felt them whenever I went to the bathroom?! No answer, no answer, no answer. But there was one guide with whom I'd developed a strong connection and with whom I was able to communicate by feeling his presence and paying attention to my thoughts. I didn't realize it at the time but I was beginning to learn about clairsentience (clear feeling) and claircognizance (clear thinking).

In the first or second of my weekly readings, Elizabeth – already managing a room full of "my team" – looked at one point as though she was peering through a crowd and said, in a very warm, welcoming, and gentle manner, like one might entice a shy puppy to come a little closer, "It's okay. Come on in. Really. Hi there." And she essentially described three little old ladies, emphasis on the little. One of them was carrying a casserole or something hot from the oven and Elizabeth was all smiles as she engaged them. It didn't take too long to figure out that this was my grandmother – the one who had made her transition before I was two – and her two sisters – both of whom I actually knew (one into my early teens and the other into my mid-twenties). Neither of my great aunts broke five feet in height and one of them was always cooking. They came that time and have appeared at virtually every reading I've had with Elizabeth since then – during that initial year and a half

right up to and including today. Usually they are just observing
the proceedings and sometimes they have interesting insights,
like when they told me that they knew the baby my friend had
just had and that yellow would help to soothe her (it did) and
after seeing me with this baby, asked me about having children
of my own, encouraging me to do so (I didn't). And sometimes
I chat with them about various family members, all of whom
I've told that I've spoken to their "dead" mother/aunt/
grandmother and all of whom, I'm quite sure, think I'm nuts.
Big fun.

In subsequent years I would have other readings with
Elizabeth "as needed," and also a smattering of non-Elizabeth
experiences like with the tiny woman in North Carolina who
channeled my uncle who had crossed over a decade earlier.
Channelers can align their energy such that the non-physical
being can literally talk through them, no "interpreter" necessary.
It was surreal to be talking with my uncle, hearing language and
attitude that were unmistakably his through a heavy Japanese
accent that was unmistakably hers. That conversation was
rather informative and actually brought me closer to him.

∞

All of this is to say that by the time Duder and I began life as
a couple, I had accumulated tons of stories about conversations
with the other side and I frequently regaled him with them. A
couple of months into our second year together, a new friend
appeared on the scene who channeled a great number of different
ascended masters, angels, and archangels and for a while there,
virtually every conversation I had with her was a conversation
with the other side and this continued when she stayed with

us for a couple of weeks. I was over the moon, walking tall, and charged up from all the high-vibration encounters. One day, Duder joined us for a lengthy conversation with the three of us and a number of "them." Afterward, when he and I were alone, he cracked some really funny jokes about it all and a day or two later made an appointment of his own with Elizabeth.

If he had never wanted to see a "psychic" or any such thing it would have been fine with me. Hard to imagine, maybe, difficult to understand, perhaps, but fine. Sure. Whatever. Yet I could see such potential for healing if he did. He had just completely changed his life by moving to a new place, embarking on a new relationship, beginning a new career, and was working, at the time, on breaking free from old habits and old ways of thinking, pretty standard stuff for a man in his mid-thirties. And as someone who loved him a lot and knew him pretty well and is generally tuned in to this sort of thing, it seemed that some unprocessed material from the experience of having lost his brother years earlier was calling for attention.

I couldn't help but be excited for what might unfold in Duder's first session with Elizabeth and knowing how very personal readings can be, I didn't want to pry. (Well I wanted to, but I didn't.) Yet when he returned he was more than willing to talk about it even though there wasn't, surprisingly, much to say. His brother had definitely shown up, but the communication wasn't as dynamic or enlightening as any of us thought it would be given the strength of their bond and the nature of their relationship. Elizabeth said that Ron was holding a shield throughout the session and she couldn't get a handle on what that meant. Sometimes it just goes that way.

A week or so later Duder was diagnosed with stage four colon cancer and we were told that it had already metastacized to his liver – also stage four. The prognosis was, as they say, grim. When Elizabeth came to the hospital as Duder was recovering from emergency surgery, we could see how the shield now made sense: there was a barrier between what he (Ron) knew and what he could say. Usually when things don't make sense in a reading, they do somewhere down the road.

For the first seven months after his diagnosis we didn't believe Duder would leave this plane. He chose an "alternative" treatment plan in Tijuana, Mexico, was extremely strong going into it, and we had every reason to be optimistic. But eventually there was a turning point and we both knew he would likely not survive. We came home from his last hospital stay and Elizabeth wanted to come over right away. She told Duder that she had a message for him from his brother and the message was that when the time came, he would be warmly welcomed on the other side and there would even be a big party. Yes, a party. Duder was quite weak at this point, but as long as he had breath in him my metaphysically-obsessed psychotherapist self would be asking questions. He basically said he was comforted by his brother's message and wanted to believe it, he just wasn't sure he could. I also asked him when he thought the time for his grand exit would arrive and he said that although he was resigned and ready, his body would probably last a few months. It lasted one.

∞

When our relationship began, Duder had been living in San Francisco and had a large collection of close friends there.

Before that, he lived in Chicago where he was born and raised. The question was, where did he want to die? His answer was at home, his new home, with me. "Really? Are you sure? I'll go wherever you want and I won't leave your side." "Really. Here, at the beach, our home, with you." It was a tremendous privilege and an awesome responsibility – a responsibility I took very seriously. Yes, he was dying. But what did that mean? To me it meant that a soul was leaving its body and it was my job to help it. Oh, and what the hell did I know about helping souls leave their bodies?

Intuitively it seemed that copious amounts of peace and quiet were called for. Profound peace and blissful quiet and, oh yes, love. Lots and lots and lots of love. So that was the mission: to let the love and light and peace and calm and quiet and tranquility overpower and drown out any and all intrusions that came from tending to his physical needs, the medical mumbo jumbo stuff, and juggling all manner of visitors from near and far. One afternoon, while some of his friends from out of town were visiting, he called me over and whispered that he wanted them all to leave. When playing good cop, bad cop I'm usually the good one but so much for that. After they left, I asked him what was up because it didn't appear that he was particularly tuckered out at the moment – something I'd monitored like a twisted combination of Jewish mother on crack and gustapo infused with a healthy dose of Zen, making sure not only that his needs were being met, but that visitors weren't putting undue strain on him. When he told me it was because he wanted us to have "our routine," I almost melted on the spot.

Prior to that moment, I didn't realize it had a name. But there was no doubt that just a few days into what would be his last month here, evenings had, indeed, become truly treasured time. All I cared about during those weeks was whether or not he was as comfortable and as happy as he could be and it meant the world to me that "our routine" meant so much to him. The routine, such as it was, included sharing dinner, at least while he was still eating something. We'd watch the sunset, like usual, then the fun really began. I'd light a ton of candles, put on some new-agey, high-vibration music, re-prepare the bed, and give him a lengthy, luxurious massage. Every night. In fact, this was the only part of the routine that lasted until his last day here. Sometimes I would read to him from some of our favorite spirituality books and sometimes we'd just lie down together. No television. No movies even. We talked about how much we loved each other and how we always expected to get married some day, various state and federal laws notwithstanding. One time I asked him how he felt about leaving me. One of his responses was that I should go with him, the other was that I'd be fine. Thanks, Duder. As it happened, "our routine" was also instrumental in restoring any peace and quiet that would inadvertently escape during the daytime hours and melt away any leftover stress and worry and fear that might have lingered in the wakes of those who inadvertently brought them. I understood why he'd wanted his friends to leave that day.

A soul was leaving its body! Holy crap! When others would observe this or that change in his eating or drinking or sleeping or breathing or energy or any of the myriad medical details available for focusing on, I would observe that he – the soul part of him – was simply spending less and less time in his body, stretching beyond it to peek at where he would be going and maybe even having some communications? Sometimes I'd notice him looking off into the distance and would pounce – lovingly and gently of course – with "Who was that?" "What did you see?" "What are they saying?" He knew that "stuff was going on," but didn't seem to have a strong handle on it and, hard as it may be to believe, I really didn't push it. At this point, he had very little strength and it was decreasing by the day.

The quest for peace and quiet and calm and tranquility was being challenged a little bit by some funky electricity issues in the house. I'd learned a while back that one of the ways non-physicals can get our attention is by affecting electrical currents and making themselves known in lights, radios, tv's, telephones, computers, etc. I hadn't had any personal experience with this particular method nor did I want to. Enamored as I am of all things metaphysical, something about messing with electricity is just annoying and it was annoying now, when we were at home all the time and wanting peace and quiet, to have lights and music and a refrigerator with important medication in it flickering on and off at will. But whose will? What was the message? Were they talking to Duder? Was there something he/we needed to know? My metaphysical sleuthing, such as it was, yielded no results. I really had no idea what I was doing but apparently the electrician did: he found and fixed the "real" problem.

Still, the experience inspired some conversation. This time we were in bed, nose to nose, talking about my failed attempts at figuring out who might be trying to communicate with him/us when I asked him, "How will I know it's you?" referring, of course, to when he would be on the other side and I would still be here, knowing that I'd want to decipher his energy from the many other non-physicals whose presences I'd been blessed to feel over the years. With great confidence and a clarity that belied his weakened state, he just looked at me and said, "You'll know." Classic Duder. I meant to convey to him that I was seriously considering what he'd said. Lips pursed; head nodding, slightly. "Hmmmm." On the inside, though, I was freaking out: *Are you kidding me? That's it? No "whenever you see a butterfly or a hot redhead walking down the street" or "whenever the clock strikes seven" or anything like that?* Well what did he know about it?! Except that he was so sure — particularly for someone whose belief in all this stuff was not exactly robust — and so I let it go, albeit with a stern warning: "Just don't fuck with my electricity" and we laughed. About a week later it was, for him, exit, stage right. Not twenty-four hours later, when I felt his energy fill my chest and then some, I did know. I knew absolutely. Classic Duder.

∞

He and I are hardly the first human beings in history to come together and fall in love and love being together. Blah, blah, yawn, yawn and a good thing that's not what this story is about. Nor is this a story about his cancer and how he and we dealt with it, blah, blah, blah. This story is about how our relationship continues on even though my partner, free from his 36-year-old cancer-ridden body, soul work for this lifetime completed, is what most people would call "dead." It's the story of how there are no tragedies or lives cut too short or relationships over before their time. It's the story of the contact we shared during the first year after he left and the ways in which that contact helped me to process his absence from this plane and from my physical life. It's the story of the opportunity I was given to practice what I preach and further develop my work. And, if I tell it well, it's the story of how our relationship, such as it was when he was here, was but a speck in the greater story of who he and I are.

He had just left and still I could feel him and the love we loved to be in. He had just left and I could feel that love in even deeper ways than when he was here. He had just left and we'd shared another sunset together and even added another song to the short list of those we'd considered to be "ours." He had just left and we weren't beginning something new and/or ending something old, we were – as I would come to realize – simply continuing on.

New Year's Eve
December 22, 2005 - December 31, 2005

If it seems to you that I was all business and emotionally unfazed about Duder's departure, you're probably not the only one. When he and I were in Mexico for what would be his last hospital stay and we began talking earnestly about his not surviving, when we were walking outside in the sun between the hospital and the beach (yes, they do things differently down there), he asked me if I had cried yet about any of what was happening – from the day it started – and what I thought about this new topic, the idea that he wouldn't survive.

I told him no; I hadn't cried. I may also have told him that, until that moment, it hadn't occurred to me to cry. Then I launched ever so gently into my take on the whole thing, the first time I'd heard it myself, even, and it went something like this: I love you so much and want more than anything for you to stay here and for us to share a long life of romantic partnership and I know you know that. But everything I know about life and how it works teaches me to *be present* and accept things as they are – *without judgment* – and to have *compassion* for another soul's journey by allowing that soul to have its journey without interference or *judgment* from me or anyone. Even if that journey means you will die and leave me here without you. (Bastard.) I also *believe* that *we are here for a reason* and there are no accidents and that if you are going to depart this plane it will be for your soul's highest good and I guess the reason nobody checked with me about it — because, trust me, I have far better ideas — is because on that level, on a soul level, it's really none of my business. Oh, and as it happens, soul level work is what I do so thanks for this oversize opportunity to practice what I preach. (Motherfucker.)

Clinical (except for that last part), I know. I thought about it afterward, believe me. *Couldn't you have told him that you cried your guts out in private but hid it from him because you didn't want him to worry about you or just plead with him to stay here and get all defiant about this not surviving business?* I could have but no, no way. It wouldn't have been me and he knew it. And I knew that my spiritual mumbo jumbo was at least part of what attracted him to me in the first place. Besides, conditions on the ground, if you will, with regard to his physicality were changing rapidly, daily, and that conversation quickly morphed into others and others and others.

On New Year's Eve day, nine months after his diagnosis, two and a half months after that conversation in Mexico, eleven days after he'd left, ten days after the telepathic sunset, three days after his wake, two days after his funeral and burial, and a day and a half after I'd returned home, I had my first emotional release. Uh, let me re-phrase that. I had my first emotional meltdown — complete with a loss of composure so insistent it consumed my being and kicked me in the stomach harder than I'd ever been kicked there before. Wails clearly rooted in some other dimension came through me in torrents and rendered me unrecognizable to myself. It was an event like you read about, like you see in the movies, like I am sure you have experienced yourself. It was the last day I had to get everything out of his apartment and I guess my moment had arrived.

To be perfectly honest, I was a bit relieved that it had. I mean, I knew I had it together, more or less, accepting it all as it was like a good little spirituality practitioner but no tears at all? Well I didn't have to think about that any longer. Surrounded by tons of his files and paperwork and things to give away, throw away, pack away, and move, I cried and cried and cried. And I noticed how the tears were bittersweet. The feelings of loss and emptiness were gargantuan and at the same time I was aware of how I couldn't have felt so much emptiness and loss if, when we were together, I hadn't also felt love that was so full and whole and complete. I was *grateful* for the stomach pains and the other-worldly sobbing because it reminded me of the love. *It is better to have loved and lost...*

And just for the record, couldn't he have cleaned up some of this stuff before he left? Gjeesh! I brought it up a couple of times, but he wouldn't engage. I mean we did the things we needed to do – power of attorney and that kind of stuff – but that was about it. There were no things he particularly wanted to give to particular people except his car to me. *What about all your CD's? What about your stereo? What about that thing on your desk you seem to like so much?* I was reaching, to be sure. *What about your prized tiger blanket?* Nope. Not interested. Didn't care. One of the things I loved about him was that he wasn't attached to things and he hardly had any. So I knew this day would come, it was here, I was in it, it was almost over, and it was fine.

Elizabeth called late in the afternoon and invited me over just to chill out, talk, and maybe meditate together. I hadn't seen her since the day before Duder left and it was the perfect invitation. I felt completely drained and I knew that sharing time with her would be easy and comfortable and there's really nothing else I would have acquiesced to doing that evening, other than keep my own company. We didn't mention anything about talking to Duder and I hadn't had anything in particular happen since the telepathic sunset experience. It was enough to be in a place of just beginning to kind of get used to how it was going to be with us, communication-wise. Also, I don't like to be presumptuous with anyone, least of all my medium friend. So when the time was right, I'd call her and make an appointment and pay the fee for an "official" reading. Tonight was not that time. Or so I thought.

I guess when one of your very close friends is a medium and your partner has just made his transition and your medium friend knew and loved your partner, too, and she can, with seemingly no effort at all, tune in to all manner of activity on the other side of the veil, things just happen. We were talking about him and she just said, "Should we see what's going on?" *Are you kidding me? Yes! Of course! Please! Absolutely!* "Sure. If you're up for it." And there they were. She and I had been seated on different couches arranged in an L configuration. She was about in the middle of hers, to my right, and I was about in the middle of mine and she said that Duder was just to my right – with his brother. In fact, they showed themselves as being in a tight embrace and two of Duder's guides were there, too, behind him.

Rapid conversation ensued. Ron was with him, for support and so they could be together, but Duder did all the talking. I was so curious about where he was in his transition process and one of the first things Elizabeth noted and told me was that his energy was fairly light — relative to most of the beings she sees. It was clear that this was because he was still so early in his transition, not quite sure-footed, as it were, but most certainly wholly present. There was no confusion on his part about where he was or what he was doing like a lost soul or anything like that. And now that we were underway, I had a zillion questions. How are you? What are you "doing?" Are you reviewing your life? Have you reunited with other family members? Are you catching up with spiritual friends who were not in this life? Is it like that book, *Journey of Souls?* Are you in a class or school? Are the guides with you guides you had before? Were they there when you made your transition? Do you miss your body? Being here? What do you know now that you didn't before? Do you know about previous lives we've had together? Have you seen God? Well? Well? Well?

What I got was: "Keep the stereo." I'm not kidding. The first thing he said to me was "keep the stereo." "Uh, but I don't want it. Or need it." The truth was I had planned to give it to a friend of ours, the same friend who was moving into his apartment the next day. She didn't have one; it was a nice thing to do; it was one less thing to move. "You keep it." Like Ron with the shield that time, sometimes things that make no sense in a session will make sense later on and so I let it go. "Okay." I was incredulous that this was what we were talking about because it seemed like such a colossal waste of time. *Are you fucking kidding me?!* But I wasn't exactly in a position to argue. There were just some things he wanted to say and it was fascinating for me to see how engaged he was in all of this earthly stuff now. Now!

To be fair, he also made a point to apologize for having left me with all of it, acknowledging that he could have done more about it himself while he was still here. The car needed to be smogged and re-registered and the power of attorney was messed up and there were tons of files with people's social security numbers on them from his work and stuff like that. Not that he could have physically done much of anything, but he could have guided the process and answered some questions. I appreciated what he was saying and said so and was still eager to move on. It just seemed like partners in love and recently separated by the veil would have more to talk about.

Then again, if he wanted to hang out at this level of discourse in the zone of minutiae, I could always address the minor but not really minor issue of his blanket. It's a very well-made, large, throw-type blanket, about 4'x6' and the reversible design on it is basically like a photo of a tiger walking toward you with a giant head and face. His grandmother used to call him Tiger and he had lots of them in various forms and when he moved to the beach, this blanket was a prominent and oft-used favorite possession of his. I can't remember ever having had one myself that I cared anything about, but he sure did. During the months of his illness, it became more and more prominent. I brought it to him in two different hospitals and it was ever-present during his last month at home.

Now anyone who has known me for a while will tell you that cats – domestic and otherwise – have always been creatures with which I have had a rather distant relationship.

Alright, they creep me out. (Bless their hearts.) Especially their faces. And before he left the only thought I had about that blanket was who I would give it to since he didn't care to "assign" it to anyone. But now that he was gone it had pretty much become the only *thing* of his I cared anything about. It was infused with his energy and I was loving wrapping myself in it and having it in the house. Suddenly, however, there was competition.

I had just received an email from his parents asking for a few things, an email I welcomed as I had asked them to be specific about anything of his they wanted from his place, particularly since they had just spent a week there. (The blanket was at my place.) There were very few things on the list but the tiger blanket was one of them and I didn't know what to do. I typically would have just deferred and given it to them, but I really wanted it for myself, which I didn't realize until they asked for it. The thought of it sitting in an empty room somewhere in their home in Chicago was not working for me one bit, yet if they had a particular plan for it, well, that would be hard to argue with. And, still, it seemed so trivial a conversation that I didn't even want to have it, but I had to answer them and it was sure was handy to be able to ask Duder what he thought. He said I should keep it, no question. He was emphatic about it, actually, so fortified with his blessing, I emailed his parents and told them all the reasons I wanted to keep it and then said I wouldn't resist if there was something specific they had in mind for it. It would have been way more fun just to say, "Steve said I could have it, so there!" But that would never fly so I went with the more standard approach. They were most gracious and told me to enjoy it.

The blanket conversation gave way to a larger conversation about my contact with his parents going forward. What should I do? What did he want me to do? We had just shared an astonishingly intimate experience that one might think would bond us to each other for life – the last week of their son's/my partner's life. It was the culmination of a relationship they never wanted to have that had begun nine months earlier in a most surreal way at a time when, like so many parents, they were struggling to accept the gay aspect of their son who, unbeknownst to them, had just landed in the hospital, was diagnosed with cancer in the emergency room, had eighty percent of his colon removed, and, for all intents and purposes, had been handed a death sentence. And it was a time when they were far from wanting anything at all to do with any *partner* their son had told them he was with and intended to stay with. "Hello, Mrs. Lewis (his father was not at home). Yes, hi, I'm Steven. We're in the hospital. I've been here all along. Yes, of course, I'll tell you everything." Emergency. Diagnosis. Surgery. Metastasis. Prognosis. (Her taking notes.) Nice to meet you. He had handed me the phone after a very groggy, "Hi Mom…I'm in the hospital…I had an operation…I have cancer…Hold on."

I picked her up at the airport a few days later and, of course, we went directly to the hospital, about a 15 or 20 minute drive. I parked the car and as we were walking inside, she asked me flat out if I would mind if Duder was buried next to his brother. If you count our chatting while driving from the airport to the hospital as one conversation and chatting while walking from the car into the hospital as another one, then this was our third conversation. Stunned, I said that I would not get in the way of anything like that, but she had to know that her son was determined to put this behind him and not go the way of his brother and that I was with him a thousand percent. Two minutes later we walked into his room and he was beyond thrilled to see her.

During her four-day (or so) stay, she was subjected not only to us as a couple, showing affection and calling each other Duder every two seconds, but also to many of our friends including, but certainly not limited to, some men who happen to be gay. And then there was the healer brigade, friends of various stripes who had rallied to his side to offer all manner of post-surgical, cancer-eliminating treatments. On several occasions we had cleared out the nurses, turned off the fluorescents, had meditations, and sometimes two or three practitioners working on him at a time, employing various energetic techniques from Reiki to QiGong to Zenith and more. Crystals, candles, aromatherapy, organic food, the works. Did I mention his mom is a nurse? Still, she wanted to be there for every such "session" and she was. I remember holding her hand a lot during those days and when she left, she told me she felt as though she'd had a spiritual experience. She also said I'd get extra points from her husband because I'd walked her into the airport and sat with her until she had to be at the gate for her flight home.

Duder was released a week or so later and we when we got home, his father was there. Nice to meet *you*. He stayed for about a week (at a hotel two blocks away) and saw us operate as a couple. He accompanied us to several appointments including one or two with my homeopath/ energy medicine doctor/friend and one or two with some of the other practitioners who had already begun to work on him in the hospital. Hardly his usual thing. He was there when we launched into full research mode to help Duder figure out what treatment approach to take and he watched me tend to Duder's foot-long incision by cleaning it and re-dressing it once or twice a day. He heard me being interviewed on a health and spirituality radio program about the work I do and peppered throughout the week, of course, were drop-ins from plenty of friends, gay and otherwise, hugging and kissing as they came and went. This mid-western ex-military, ex-police officer man in control went along with the program every step of the way and while I don't think he would have called it a spiritual experience, I did get a big hug when I dropped him off at the airport.

Still, it didn't feel to me as though their separate baptisms-by-fire necessarily endeared us all to one another in any significant way. Duder certainly loved having us all together and we were more than cordial and friendly whenever we shared space and time during the months between his diagnosis and his departure. But I pick up on energy and from my perspective, no amount of polite conversation could ever have compensated for the epic energetic mismatch that Duder and his cancer – the center of it all – had attracted to himself in his parents and me, particularly during the last week of his life when we spent seven or eight hours a day together every day. Truthfully? It was – *energetically speaking* – like some sort of psycho, gay-straight, traditional-alternative, parent-child version of Mars and Venus in the cancer ward. There was religious Catholic energy and new-agey Jewish energy. There was energy aligned with expression of feeling and energy aligned with suppression of feeling. There was energy aligned with conventional medicine and energy aligned with myriad alternatives to it. There was energy aligned with life after death and reincarnation and energy not aligned with that at all. There was energy aligned with a blaring military television channel as acceptable background noise while someone was dying and energy aligned with airy music and silence for the same occasion. There was energy aligned with the death and loss of a second son and energy aligned with easing the journey for a beloved partner. There was the energy of love and fear and acceptance and grief and compassion and dread and hope and anger and all of it – all of it – was swirling around Duder and throughout my very small house like some invisible tornado whipping itself inside a hurricane on the blackest of days that only I seemed privy to. I could and did handle a lot but that dynamic almost did me in, so much so that I *had* to talk about it with his parents and I did. Afterward, I felt better for a good two or three minutes. The only real way out was for me to leave and that wasn't going to happen or for them to leave and that wasn't going to happen either. But this was Duder's deal and I was just a witness.

So back to the original questions. What should I do? What did Duder want me to do? Without him in the picture and with nothing else connecting me to his parents, what was there for us? This was the one and only time his brother said something and he and Duder were in complete agreement: I didn't need or have to do anything. Zilch. Nada. I was under no obligation, as far as either of them were concerned, to maintain any level of communication with Duder's parents or his sister and her family (whom I'd met a couple of times, but not spent nearly as much time with). I was a bit surprised because I thought there would be some of that *please look out for them* kind of stuff, but there wasn't any. And it was interesting to me that they were both so clear and definite about it.

When it came to me and his parents, the differences in our worldviews were stark and they collided at the junction of Duder — their son, my partner — at a time of ridiculously high anxiety and emotional vulnerability. Now their deceased sons had granted me complete freedom from any kind of responsibility toward them and right then and there everything in me said that any future contact would have to be *their* choice and at whatever level they desired. I was super sensitive about not insinuating myself or being the salt rubbing their wounds; I didn't want to be tolerated when they'd perhaps prefer not to have any contact at all (but would never say so); and I certainly didn't want to seem as though I was doing anything that might be construed as trying to take the place of their son. I was relieved to be free from obligation and was happy to let it all unfold as it was going to.

So we'd covered his stereo, the blanket, and my emergent relationship with his family, but I was just getting going. Could we do more? I was checking with Elizabeth and with Duder and got the green light. Alrighty then. So what about that party, by the way? Did it happen? Yep, it sure did. But not quite the way we thought and here's another peek into how information received doesn't always precisely translate no matter how skilled the translator. If you remember, Ron had asked Elizabeth to tell Duder that there would be a big party for him when he crossed over. The day before he left, Monday, Elizabeth predicted he would go on Saturday because she was shown the party and it was on Saturday. But he left the next day, on Tuesday. Elizabeth's prediction that Duder would leave on Saturday was based on her assumption that the party would happen pretty much upon his arrival "over there," an assumption "they" didn't correct. Oh those crazy non-physicals, keeping the mysteries alive.

Then it occurred to me to ask him about the book I'd been working on. "Are you going to help me with my book from over there? Help get it published? Help pave the way?" I was pretty surprised when he demurred and told me that he was really quite a procrastinator and I probably shouldn't count on him for much of that. *Excuse me?!* It was a spontaneous question on my part, not something I'd consciously thought about before, but his response was still a bit surprising given how incredibly supportive of it he was when he was here. I chalked it up to "not his department" and moved on.

So have you ever thought about going to your own funeral? Duder went to his. And to his wake. And to his burial. And to the luncheon afterward. Apparently it's an option. He had several observations about it all including the fact that, according to him, he didn't have quite as many cars in his processions from the funeral home to the church and the church to the cemetery as his brother had had. This was actually something he *did* think about before he crossed over and even talked with his mother about, such that one family of five, their neighbors and very close friends, actually drove in five separate cars. So here was Duder being typical Duder, having fun competing with his brother – on the other side – over whose funeral procession was bigger. We also talked about how surreal it was for me to have been at his home in Chicago, the house he grew up in, in his world, surrounded by his immediate and extended family and the friends and neighbors he'd known all his life – all the people he'd wanted me to meet, which I did, without him there. Except, of course, he was there.

Then I saw a glimpse of a more serious, more ethereal version of Duder when I questioned the value of some of what I'd just experienced in Chicago, particularly the wake. I was more than familiar with the concept and had been to many in my life. (I grew up in a town very much dominated by Catholics and many of my closest friends were and are Catholic.) But I never really understood what people got out of wakes and while I'm sure I thought I was being utterly *non-judgmental*, I probably wasn't. He didn't scold or lecture me or anything remotely close to that, but it was clear now that he embodied a reverence for all of it that I had never experienced in him before and he was conveying a sense that there was far more to any of it than I knew. Duder as angel? Spiritual teacher? I was definitely not ready for that.

Next up, Elizabeth was looking kind of perplexed and was asking, "Lots of white flowers?" Her question had an air of *Where did that come from?* to it. Meanwhile, my mind had drifted for a moment to the memorial service I had decided to have for Duder at the beach the following week and though I hadn't planned anything out yet, at all, I did have the thought to somehow use a bunch of white flowers. So he was parroting my thought back to Elizabeth! Fun thing about readings sometimes – "they" don't always wait for us to use words. "What?!," I exclaimed after she'd mentioned the white flowers. "Are you kidding me?" I began to rant because I thought he was attempting to direct the plans for his memorial service from there, but that wasn't the case. He was just having fun. Same old Duder. Again.

I also noticed something else. In this short time, he had gained a much deeper understanding of and respect for his father. He'd always gotten on quite well with his mom but had a more challenging relationship with his dad. In this session, his tone about his father had also changed considerably and, combined with his tone about the church, was giving me a real insight into how the part of us that goes on, the soul part, is continually working on its growth and development. It does so while here on Earth in human form and it does it over there when no longer in human form. As above, so below. I got to see this because I'd made a crack about his dad or really about him and his dad, one that, typically, he'd have laughed at, and Elizabeth's face told me something was awry. "He's not thinking that way anymore," she said. "He knows things now he didn't used to know and he understands more." He was healing his relationship with his father – from over there. Free of his body and his human-ness, he was no longer in a place of making *judgments.* This from a man whose judgment-making skills were well-honed when he was here. Oy.

Moving on, I was very curious to know what Duder had to say about who was with him when he actually drew his last breath because before it happened, a lot was said on our side of the situation. Well almost. Because even though I'm usually Mr. Let's Talk About It, there was one conversation I was working hard not to have with anybody. It was 7:00 on the seventh day of his parents' stay with us – three hours past cut-off for "our routine" – and they were getting ready to leave for the evening. First, though, they called me onto the deck – out of earshot from Duder – and asked me if I thought he was going to make it through the night. *Excuse me?* He had been conscious and mostly sleeping all day and for whatever it was worth and why ever I thought so, I didn't think this was going to be his last night. And as I was saying all that, I realized that what we were really talking about was being at his side when the time arrived. The conversation I didn't want to have.

Selfishly, I always hoped that he and I would be alone, I'd be holding him, and he'd go. But my *belief* was that it was going to go down the way it was going to go down based on what would serve his highest good, not my ego's desire. And so I was adamant about not attempting to choreograph anything because to do so felt like venturing into waters that were none of my concern, none of anybody's concern, really, except his and God's. And I knew without them saying it that his parents very much wanted, likely expected, to be with him because when their other son left this world, he did so when nobody was in the room and they have lived with the regret of that for more than a dozen years.

I took a deep breath and told them flat out there was no way they could stay at the house 24/7. Tornado in a hurricane. Then I reminded them that Duder could slip away while I was asleep next to him and I wouldn't even know. I spared them my speech about it not being our business, then I offered some concessions. I promised them that starting that night, I would keep both phones in bed with us. If I noticed anything at all at any time during the night, I would call them immediately and they could be here in two minutes. And I told them that if they woke up at any point and wanted to know anything at all whatsoever, to call me regardless of the time. I then suggested they go to dinner and invited them to come back at around 9:00. "Really?" "Yes, of course," I said. (I'm not a monster.)

They left and I crawled into bed with Duder. Ahhh. No, really. Ahhhhhh. This was why we'd been having "our routine," our time to re-connect and re-group, and I had missed those last three hours. I started to say something to him and then thought better of it, knowing that this was a moment far beyond words. He was lying on his back and I snuggled up nice and close, my face and body against his, and took his hand in mine. Breathing. Being. Reveling. Absorbing. Perfection. At precisely 9:00, there was a knock on the door and our blissful time together came to a screeching halt. When his parents came in, the energy contrast was staggering. Kind of like it always was, the contrast that is, but more pronounced somehow. I wanted to protect Duder from it, but that certainly wasn't my place and I wasn't even sure I could. I went into the other room, such as it was. With only a half wall separating the living room from the bedroom, I could get to where nobody was in my line of sight by sitting at the table a few more feet away almost, but not quite, elbow-on-table, chin-in-hand, eyes rolling, foot tapping. Almost.

After about ten minutes his father called me over. Urgently. "Steven!" I walked over to them. "Was he breathing like this before?!" I leaned over and "checked" and couldn't quite tell. It didn't seem that different to me, I said so, and I went back to where I had been. I was just waiting for them to leave so he and I could be alone again and I had no idea how long that would be. At 9:30, he did it again. "Steven! This is it!" *What?!* I went back and they were bracing themselves. With Duder still lying on his back and under the blankets, his mom was kind of by his knees and thighs, his dad was by his waist and stomach, and they had made room for me to be aligned with his chest and head. Awkward, I thought, the whole scene, but oh yeah, this wasn't about me. I got with the program and quickly re-focused my energy, did a 180, really, leaned over, my right arm brushing his father's left, looked right at Duder, and repeated over and over in my mind: *Go with God, go with peace, go with light, go with love, go with joy, go with courage, go with grace, go with…, go with…, go with…* and I didn't let up on repeating that loop until, at 9:39, his father said, "That's it." "Huh?" It was like being yanked out of a trance and I said, "Really?" And he was right. Duder had stopped breathing.

We didn't choreograph anything and we were all there when it happened. That's because it had been "choreographed" not by human Duder in his very weakened state, but by his higher self. And he told me why it went down the way it did. The presence of his parents served the function of providing a level of comfort to him as, armed with a certain amount of fear and trepidation, he approached the moment he would leave his body. They were his parents, after all. But more than that, he told me, was that his higher self in essence gifted *them* with that experience for the healing properties it would engender with regard to both their sons. Having been there for Steve would make their overall mourning process a bit gentler but also, because *everything is energy*, everything affects everything, it would contribute to healing the heartache they'd carried for more than a dozen years with specific regard to not having been physically present when Ron made his transition.

My presence, he told me, was really the inverse of that. It was not so much for me because he knew I would navigate through my "mourning process" whether I was there when he left or not. Rather, he said, my being there was really more for him because I was able, in that moment of time, to anchor and be a conduit for a lighter, higher-frequency of energy that could transcend the more dense – and utterly understandable – energy of his parents and help him on his way. The *"go with..."* loop really, truly, helped! And what that loop was, in essence, was prayer. Prayers work because *everything is energy* and we shape that energy and direct it with our thoughts and I was directing a lighter energy to him in the hopes that it would ease his transition and it did. And I was blessed to know it. Holy crap!

You'd think that would have been enough but I had one more little question. I told him that as we are wont to do when people "die," I had said to anyone who asked about it that he'd "gone peacefully." But did he really? I asked him to describe everything he could about the actual moment he crossed over while his parents and I were at his side and then the first moments "over there" while I was on the phone with the mortuary and the hospice people and emailing our friends and relatives, while his father was making phone calls, and while his mother stood by his body. When I was asking my questions about believing that Duder had "gone peacefully," Elizabeth's face lightened and a full, knowing smile with a hint of intrigue and a sense of wonder appeared. Actually, it was joy. Her face reflected pure joy. Duder was saying that he didn't quite have the words to describe and convey the splendor and brilliance of the experience.

But he did use the word *mist* and was saying it was as if he had *misted* out of his body into a warm, familiar, and all-encompassing state of love. There was no white light for him, but he was welcomed immediately by two very loving guides who were very familiar to him and within minutes he was reuinted with Ron, his grandmother, and other souls known to him. On this side of the veil, we see a lifeless but solid, intact body. But Duder was saying that from the other side, from the soul's perspective, because it is leaving a body it will never again inhabit, it's as if it breaks apart, disintegrates, and falls away – no longer relevant or of value.

Elizabeth's face again. She suddenly took on a look of concern and questioning. Something like, "Wait, where are you going? What happened?" Duder's energy was fading and I could certainly understand. We'd been conversing for an hour or so, maybe more, and there was so much back-and-forth and he was so unaccustomed to everything – being away from here, being there, communicating in this way, walking between the worlds. I certainly didn't want to tax him and he said he wanted to stay, but didn't want to talk any more. That was fine because, guess what? My grandmother and both her sisters were there. Of course they were. Elizabeth's focus was now more straight ahead for her, past me and to my left where the three of them had gathered.

The first thing I did was to ask if they all knew each other, the three of them and Duder, and they didn't. So if you can imagine this scene, I basically introduced my very recently deceased partner and his brother – who I never knew – to my grandmother – who I never knew – and her two sisters, all of whom were on the other side. That was a trip. My grandmother and great aunts acknowledged that yes, indeed, I had certainly chosen well, because I'd asked them what they thought of "my man." Then my attention went to them. They are usually relatively timid and, as I think I said before, tend to stay in the background during readings. But this was different as my grandmother said that there were things I needed to know about my mother, her daughter. Now? She was persistent and we embarked on what was a relatively lengthy discussion about my mom – the greatest relationship challenge I've had in this lifetime. My grandmother endeavored to provide me with valuable perspective about her and while I was sure it all made sense somewhere, something about what she was telling me just wasn't making its way into my being. Maybe I was just too exhausted to take it all in, I wasn't sure. Her words rang in my ears, though, for weeks and months to follow. Duder and Ron stayed throughout that conversation and when my grandmother was finished, I thanked everyone profusely for the time and the company and the love and the conversation. I especially thanked Elizabeth for facilitating so generously.

∞

A new year was upon us and I was just barely beginning to process what I realized were actually two separate, if overlapping, experiences. One was the absence of my partner from this plane and living life without him and the other was the experience of having helped a soul to leave its body. I wasn't quite sure what it was I would do, but I was beginning to have some ideas about what I wasn't going to do. I wasn't going to listen to what the psychologists said *(there are five stages to grief and loss you must go through; don't make any major decisions while you are in mourning; the mourning process is roughly 18 months for every five years together)*; I wasn't going to listen to what the Jews said *(11 months of mourning with restrictions on activities and prescriptions for when it's appropriate to partner again)*; I wasn't going to listen to what my friends the Catholics said *(well I didn't really know what they said, but I wasn't going to listen anyway)*; I wasn't going to listen to what conventional wisdom said *(this is really hard; you never get over it)*; and I certainly wasn't going to listen to what the calendar said *(it's always harder on birthdays, anniversaries, deathdays)*. I was determined to engage this process on my own, in my own way, on my own terms, and as I saw fit.

And how could I do otherwise? So much of what people typically thought and said just didn't match my experience. *He went too soon.* Actually, he went right when he planned to. *It's such a tragedy.* No such thing. *At least he went peacefully.* You have no idea. *This is going to be really hard.* I'll get back to you on that. *He'd want you to stay in touch with his parents.* Guess again. *You poor thing.* Don't say that. *I can't believe he's dead.* He's not. Just ask him.

He had had a peaceful and loving transition. He was warmly welcomed and even celebrated on the other side. He was joyful. He was himself…and then some. And I didn't have to guess about any of it.

Memorials and Moving
January 1, 2006 – February 28, 2006

Between New Year's Eve and the end of February, I had one "official" reading with Elizabeth and a couple of unofficial ones and a super unofficial one when she mentioned, pretty much in passing, that Duder had been there during the memorial service I'd had for him (for me) on the beach. It was a sunny and warm Sunday morning, January 8, and about 40 of us gathered in a circle on the sand for a homemade ceremony that would last a little more than an hour. Typical stuff. We burned sage and invoked the four directions and lit a candle in a hurricane glass to stand for Duder; we read messages from people who couldn't be there and also some inspirational passages from various sources; we held white flowers which we placed in a large vase after speaking our memories of him; we played some music and hugged each other and then headed back to my house for a reception (which, on any other day, would have been called a party).

I strived for an upbeat tone but, still, I think most everyone there stood with his or her own version of somber mood and thoughts about how we shouldn't even be here and how sad it all was that this wonderful 36-year-old man would have to die so soon from such a relentless disease and how awful it was for his poor parents and his sister and the rest of his family and how lonely it was for his friends and how heartbreaking it was for this other wonderful man (that would be me) whom he had partnered with and who would now be deprived of the elation of their relationship. I felt all that. And no doubt a very significant number of those thoughts recalled and connected to other similar thoughts from experiences and stories we all have about cancer and death and sadness and grief and loss. And damn if he wasn't right there the whole time, inside our circle, kneeling in the sand like a kid by the tree on Christmas morning, beaming, and soaking it all up. Unbelievable. Utterly, believable. I wondered then – and I still do – what that morning might have been like if all of us could have seen Duder as Elizabeth did.

He was not somber or sad or grief-stricken or anything close to it. He was, according to my dear friend, as we'd already experienced him a couple of times since he'd left – quite joyful. There was no doubt that he was home, in a place that seemed to be so much like what we've read and heard and wondered about – even hoped for – a place of unconditional love, unlimited support, and unbounded joy. Yet when he joked about how there *could* have been more people and more flowers (are you seeing a pattern here?), he was showing how very connected he still was to the life he had just left behind. I didn't know if his being here was playtime or part of his work or both, or if it was just because he was missing me as much as I was missing him or what. Regardless, it was intriguing and mysterious and stimulating and wonderful and comforting, genuinely comforting, and I was loving it. Yet his being in both places, as it were, there *and* here, was certainly getting in the way of my boo-hooing the "fact" that he wasn't here and, as such, was confusing the whole "grief and loss" thing we supposedly enter when we "lose a loved one."

True enough, I was beginning to get it about loss. I'd already experienced how I could be humming along one moment and be doubled over the next, confounded by the irony that the very absence of something, the feeling of inflated, empty, space, could produce a physical ache. So he could dance around in the ethers all he wanted but there was no getting around the fact that he was gone, no longer here, no longer someone I could hold and be held by and nobody could talk me out of that feeling by telling me there, there, he's not *really* gone, he'll live on in your heart forever, barf. I was getting it about loss because I was *feeling* it. But grief? I couldn't feel grief. Life had taught me the phrase, "grief and loss" and graduate school reinforced it plenty. I lived with people who had experienced it and worked as a therapist with people who had experienced it and I wasn't experiencing it, not all of it. One order of grief and loss, please, hold the grief?

∞

I was now pretty much done with Duder-death-and-dying projects. Obviously, there was nobody who needed 24-hour care anymore and the habit of being on hyper alert had begun to wane. (I knew that was true when I left the house one day and didn't take my cell phone with me, the first time for that in close to a year.) The car situation was settled, a lot of the business-y stuff was well under way, his apartment had been vacated, the funeral was behind me and now, so too, was the memorial service on the beach. The final event was another memorial or Celebration of Life, as it was called, the following week, in San Francisco, for which all I had to do was show up. I arrived wearing his clothes and was so warmly and lovingly welcomed by his family of friends there. They put together a wonderful afternoon and I bawled a lot, in front of everyone. First time for everything.

I felt him all over the place in San Francisco. And by that I mean I was beginning to differentiate between the garden variety "goose bumps" and "chills" and "tinglies" I so often felt and the ones I felt that were connected to him, specifically. His were distinguishable because they came with an extra wave of emotion – like a miniature version of the telepathic sunset experience when I just knew what I was feeling was him. Us. I didn't see him like Elizabeth did, though my obsession with wanting to was still going strong. It was sure nice to know, though, that wherever I was, he could make his presence known and I'd know it. But I still had some questions.

When I felt him like that, was he just saying hi? Agreeing with something I'd said? Something I'd thought? Trying to tell me something? All of the above? None of the above? I really wanted to know. Feeling him was one thing, a very pleasant one thing, but only part of what I was looking for. I wanted to be able to communicate easily and clearly, back and forth, and to know what he was saying. Perhaps I was wanting that so badly because as I was driving home from San Francisco it was painfully obvious that the proverbial slate was clean. There was absolutely nothing left on the calendar, related to him, specifically to *do* and I remember thinking that this was, without a doubt, one of those *first day of the rest of my life* moments if ever there was one. Then I asked The Light, while driving south on I-5 headed toward Los Angeles, if it was, perhaps, maybe, time to leave the beach. It wasn't a brand new idea, exactly, more like one whose time had possibly arrived. I loved the beach, no doubt about it, and in one of my very first conversations with Duder I told him that while I was in no hurry and had no particular place to go, I was feeling that, after 18 years, the beach was becoming less my home and more my home base. Little did I know, it was about to become his home and, ultimately, sharing it with him was really big fun. It never occurred to me to leave it when we were there together, but it was occurring to me now as I was driving home with my clean slate.

I contacted a realtor friend and we listed my house to see what would happen. Wham bam I accepted a final offer one week later and so, apparently, it *was* time to leave the beach. I called Duder's parents for what would be our first post-everything conversation. I knew I had plenty to talk about – reporting on the Celebration of Life in San Francisco and, hot off the presses, my impending move. His mom was home and our conversation was, for me, tender and warm. I could only wonder what it was like for her as I looked forward to more.

In the days between listing and selling the house, I also scheduled a formal, official session with Elizabeth because my inability to connect with Duder the way I wanted to, tinglies notwithstanding, was frustrating me big time. I desperately wanted some unswerving communication and, apparently, so did he. On the day of our appointment, which was scheduled for 4:00 in the afternoon, I called Elizabeth to confirm. She said that while she was walking on the beach that morning, Duder appeared and was super hyper and excited about the session. She basically waved him off and reminded him that his appointment wasn't until four. Buddy.

∞

Walking into Elizabeth's space felt to me like crawling into a warm bed after being up for two days. There was nothing else I wanted to do and nowhere else I wanted to be. In no time we were underway and a few things were immediately apparent. The first, which I'd already learned from my confirmation phone call, was how completely over the moon, excited, and very happy Duder was – in general and, in particular, to be sharing this time together. Elizabeth said he was practically jumping all over the place like earlier on the beach before settling somewhere very close to me, his arm on mine or around me or something like that. (For the record, I have yet to actually feel his presence when Elizabeth tells me that he's nestled in right next to me or anything like that. I always feel like a dad trying not to step on his kid's imaginary friend. *If you say so.*) Also, she told me that his presence, his energy, was strong and full and vibrant. What a difference three weeks had made! She said he looked really good and healthy and on the thin side, and I imagined him as he looked about a month or six weeks after his diagnosis and surgery: fifteen or twenty pounds lighter in weight, but really good, strong, and ready to take on the challenge that was before him. His brother was also with him as were his guides.

Elizabeth's face was showing tremendous recognition and she was nodding. Yep. Of course. He was feeling the exact same way I was about our communication – completely frustrated. And that right there...that sameness between us whenever it came to anything important and the imperative in each of us to, above all else, resolve and transmute any issue, big or small, that might, for any reason, blur or confuse or dampen our connection, pretty much right when it was happening, made it feel as though nothing had changed between us whatsoever.

When issues would arise one of us would ask, "What page are you on?" "Sixty four," might be the random response and the other might say, "Well I'm on 65" if it felt minor or "I'm on 97" for something more major and we'd pretty much do what we needed to do to get on the same page. Nothing was ever more important than that and we always knew we'd handle whatever came up. I already felt healed.

He definitely had some ideas about how we could communicate more smoothly. He said I should create a circle of candles on the floor large enough to comfortably contain me. *Oh brother.* Then Elizabeth told me he was showing her a scene which, as she described it, I realized was from when he had first moved to the beach. He'd been unpacking and all of that and asked me to come over in the evening. I walked in and saw immediately that he had – at the risk of sounding gayer than gay – lined the perimeter of his large, round rug with candles. He had made dinner for us and we sat on the rug, surrounded by the candles, eating and drinking and laughing and trying not to burn ourselves or set the place on fire while we celebrated his new home and our new life together.

Now he was suggesting I re-create what we unwittingly created that night: an energetic field of us. *Interesting.* He said I should call on him, light the candles, and sit, lie, or take whatever position would be most comfortable for me inside the field; he said to bring a crystal I had into the space along with some paper and a pen to write things down I wanted to communicate about; he said to place and light two more candles in the center – one for him, one for me – and not just him and me but *holy* him and *holy* me. *Now we're getting somewhere.* He was saying that it was time to connect more on the level of spirit and/or soul and/or higher self and/or whatever term one might use for it. He had been playing in my dimension for the last month, so to speak, and was now urging me to stretch a little to play in his. I was so taken not only by his demeanor, which was utterly based in the person I knew him to be and simultaneously slightly uncharacteristic, but by the whole idea of his offering spiritual instruction and the confidence with which he was doing it. I asked him if he was training to be an angel or something and he said, "That would be like calling a private a general." Modest, for sure, and not exactly a denial.

So now it was me who was over the moon and super excited because Duder used to always say that *I* was the "spiritual one" of our relationship. I was the one with the books, the knowledge, the woo-woo experiences, and the *intention* to make spirituality what I do for a living so I was the one who could teach him. And I did, but it was a two-way street because, in his soul, he was a teacher, too, and I would often tell him, much to his surprise, how much I learned just from being with him. Beyond that, though, I had a sense from the very beginning that when it came to any of this spirituality stuff, he knew infinitely more than I did about any of it, he just didn't seem to know that he knew it. Then one day he said, "Duder, let's have spiritual hour." It was one of those moments that confirmed for me that he was, in fact, the perfect partner. Spiritual hour became reading together from a book or talking about how to make spirituality a bigger part of our relationship or meditating together and stuff like that. They were fun, bonding experiences and, best of all, they weren't my idea. And now there he was, on the other side of the veil, engaged full time, or so it seemed, in spiritual pursuits. I *knew* it! What I had seen in him when he was here, that sense that he knew way more than I did about any of it, that characteristic he did not see in himself, was now something he was simply being and he was teaching and instructing *me*, which would take some getting used to. With the frustration over our communication now evaporated and a plan in place to improve it, we moved on to other things.

As the days since he left morphed into weeks, I was becoming more and more aware of the link between the absence of his body from my life and the profound feelings of loss I'd been experiencing. I knew what it was like for me to not have his physicality anymore, but I was wondering what it was like for him. And without getting too crazy, being that we had an audience and all (Elizabeth, his brother, his guides, my grandmother and great aunts, Elizabeth's guides, who knows who else), I took the opportunity, while we were on the subject, to tell him how grateful I was for the strong sexual relationship we'd always enjoyed. Elizabeth shrieked in surprise and laughter and told me that he was agreeing wholeheartedly and was making the universal sign – a man's sign anyway – for having sex: arms extended forward, fists, repeated fists-to-forward-and-back-gyrating-hips motion, and an oh yeah oh yeah facial expression for good measure. You know what I'm talking about! He said he missed it all, too – especially the sex – so I invited him to come back any time. He said he missed being in a body a little bit, somewhat, but that seemed mostly due to the fact that he hadn't left it all that long ago and that he had just been joking around about sex. Moving right along, then.

Two thoughts were swirling around in my consciousness. The first was that, one month out, he didn't seem to have any anguish whatsoever about being where he was and not being here. Not that he didn't *feel* anything, he did, like when he felt frustration about our communication or lack thereof. But it was becoming abundantly clear that there was nothing on that side of the veil equating to what we go through on this side of it grief and loss-wise. Nothing. And that really struck me.

The other (far less high-minded) thought emerging during this reading was about his brother. I knew that this being was of monumental importance to Duder and that he had been a source of great comfort to him on the other side. I wanted that for Duder as much as he wanted it for himself, genuinely, of course. Yet I was also beginning to feel a bit inhibited, in a way, by his brother's constant presence during the conversations we'd been having. Duder was so strongly connected to him, I was so strongly connected to Duder, but I felt no connection to his brother at all. None whatsoever. And I was beginning to feel as though our privacy, if you will, was being impinged upon and it was bugging me. I wasn't exactly ready to ask, "Would you mind leaving your brother at home next time?," but I was beginning to think it. No offense.

So as this "official" session was coming to a close I had some oh-by-the-way questions about my spirit guides. "Are they all still with me? Are there any new ones?" Experience had taught me that they can come and go and it had been ages since I'd specifically addressed the topic. As I did, I adjusted myself from a full-on slouch to a more respectful posture, hoping I wasn't crushing Duder in the process. I probably wouldn't even have noticed I had done so except when I looked at Elizabeth, she was doing the same thing. Her eyes were fixed straight ahead and she said that, "Yes, there's someone new here." She described a male being in somewhat regal terms. A sense of reverence came over both of us while Duder, unscathed by my fumbling and now somewhere between Elizabeth and my guide and more across from me, was all excited all over again. He'd been waiting for this, he said, and he knew this entity. This was my new guide. He had come on the scene a month ago, right after Duder had made his transition, when I'd had that expansive feeling during and after our telepathic sunset communication. And now I knew why it felt as though my soul had grown.

We had a brief, introductory conversation, my new guide and I, and when I asked how I could communicate with *him*, he suggested that I do so during my morning meditations and that, ala Duder's suggestion, to think in terms of *holiness* when I did. Not just *holy* him and *holy* me, but *holy* everything. The chair I sat on, the pillow at my back, the space I was in, the sun rising, and I said okay, no problem, and pretty much meditated with him every morning for the entire year. It's clear to me now, if it wasn't then, that his suggestions were about reminding me how *we are all connected* and what connects us is Source energy and, in that sense, every *thing* is holy, every *thing* is alive because it contains Source energy and that consciously connecting to All That Is, is a pretty good way to start the day. And that idea, for me, links right to *having an attitude of gratitude* for every thing because every thing comes from Source.

He also said it would be part of my process in the coming months, simply to *be*. No problem there. Then the three of us pretty much made an agreement: I would meditate and communicate with my guide in the early mornings (my usual meditation time) and I would have my time with Duder in the evenings (our usual sunset time) whenever I wanted to. I was self-conscious about the idea that my time with Duder would, apparently, always be on my schedule, when *I* wanted it, but he said that was perfectly okay. Curious, I asked him how many places he could be in at once and he said, directly, "four." I don't know why and it's not like I had anything to compare it to, but I was impressed with that. And then my guide told me that unlike previous years where I'd had so many different non-physical guides and teachers, he and Duder would essentially be it for me for now. My immediate reaction to that was a feeling that my safety net had suddenly been made much smaller, even though I knew it wasn't a numbers game. And for some reason, I felt a little intimidated by this being which is not a normal feeling for me. But Duder knew him and *that* was exciting and it encouraged me to trust. Oh that. And with profound gratitude to both of them and to Elizabeth, this "official" session came to a close.

∞

A few days later I signed a contract on the beach house and moving day was set for February 28. (Sorry, psychologists.) The other side of this equation was where I would go and, unlike when Duder and I first met, that was not a mystery. I knew that if it was time to leave the beach I would go to the mountains – to a little town only two hours east of the beach complete with four seasons and snow in winter. I knew it because in the time Duder and I were together, that town – a place I'd been visiting and enjoying for 15 years – had become much more of a home away from home than ever before. It all began when

I took him there for the first time early in our first summer together. I always thought I'd get a place there someday, but visiting for weekends was so easy and it just hadn't yet become a priority. Not surprisingly, Duder fell in love with the town at first sight and we started talking excitedly about the concept of having a place there in addition to our place at the beach. At *his* urging and for the first time ever for me, we even looked at houses before we left that weekend. That winter, at *my* urging, we rented one for a month to experience winter, to allow me to get a jump on my writing, and to give us the opportunity to feel out living in both places. A few months later, as spring was springing, we were still eager to get there but not yet ready to buy, so we decided to rent a house for six months to continue playing around with what it would be like to have homes in both places.

It was a perfectly timed plan. I was eager to write more and found it much easier to do up there; he was working hard not only at a new job in a new career, but on creating and establishing a life of his own at the beach separate from me and mine (a deal we had made before he moved) and a few days apart each week would support that project quite nicely; and we'd be able to be together whenever we wanted to in either of two bitchin' places. I went up and found a really great house to rent (different from the winter one) and a couple of days after negotiating the deal, he landed in the hospital and received his cancer diagnosis. One of the first post-surgical discussions we had was about abandoning the mountain house rental idea but, after a few days, that just didn't feel right. We knew his back was against the wall, medically speaking, but he had decided it wasn't going to get him and we truly believed that we would eventually put "the year Duder had cancer" behind us. Our m.o. was to live life until and unless there was a reason not to and so we took the mountain place for six months and had it for most of the time of his illness. The house was great and the property was glorious. The renting agents pretty much blocked direct contact between renters and owners so we asked them to please let us know if they ever got wind that the owners wanted to sell it, figuring they'd be the first to know.

Then it dawned on me that the beach house would only be mine for another month or so and I wanted to spend as much time in it as I could, absorbing the calm, peaceful Duder energy that still lingered. My clean slate was already dotted with a few new projects: one was packing; one was buying a new house; one was moving; and one was figuring out how to communicate regularly and clearly and evenly with Duder. Very soon after the session I just told you about, I attempted spiritual hour 2.0 with Duder and the candles and had to laugh because my house wasn't big enough for it without moving the couch! Still, I practiced variations on the theme and figured I'd have more room once I moved.

But the buying a new house project was not going so well. There was nothing on the market that remotely interested me so I went up for the weekend to see about where I could store my stuff and live while I continued house hunting. Ugh. I called the rental agents from the previous year because I wanted to let them know about Duder's having made his transition and to thank them for their kindnesses and flexibility during our rental time. And I also wanted to show the house we'd rented, if it was vacant, to a friend of mine who was also up there that weekend. The agent told me that it was funny I was calling now – about 10 weeks since I'd left – because they were just getting ready to call me. The owners wanted to sell! They had a listing ready to go and were just waiting for the current renters to leave so they could update some photos for it. I almost jumped through the phone.

Excitement, scramble, scramble, excitement, energy, offer, counter offer, energy, counter offer, me uncharacteristically hard-ass in the negotiations, then no energy. Nothing. Dead. Echo. Oh shit. Had I gone too far? Pushed too hard? Demanded too much? What was my deal anyway? I never get that way. Three days of nothing. A very long three days. Then a break in the non-action, a humble me prostrated before the realty gods and, poof, it was mine! I could move in the same day I moved out of the beach and we would close two weeks later, done deal. Phew! As far as I was concerned, one of the nicest features of the house was that Duder and I had spent time in it together, time spent during a very special time in our lives, and knowing that he knew the house made the move that much easier. Well, who was I kidding? The whole thing – from selling the beach house to buying the mountain house to moving was incredibly easy, three days of negotiating shenanigans notwithstanding.

Meanwhile, there were some other shenanigans going on. At my friend's house in mid-February, while a few of us were gathered for brunch and about to sit down to eat, we heard something which I ignored. But one of my friends looked on the floor and picked up a magnet that he saw lying there; it was the same magnet that had been holding up a picture of Duder on the refrigerator a few feet away. Then there was a somewhat more dramatic event at another friend's house, of a Christmas tree ornament of Duder's that his mom had sent our friend and that got moved from being inside the envelope it had arrived in to its hanging up by our friend's desk while he'd been at work. Hanging up! Our friend was freaking out for two days trying to get in touch with me, sure that I had been at his house. I hadn't been. I'm absolutely loathe to admit it, but with this second, grand maneuver, I was full-on jealous. Jealous! Me! Why oh why wouldn't he do things at my house? Fun things? Letting me know he was around? I mean, it's not like I wouldn't have welcomed it, for crying out loud.

Not long after both of these incidents, the guy who bought my house wanted to come over and take some measurements. No problem. I'd never met him and when he came in with a friend of his and his realtor, I was blown away by the energy that burst forth from him in all directions. It was huge. And his friend, who would be living in the studio downstairs, was not dissimilar. I wondered to myself how my old, little beach cottage would contain this guy, both these guys. Not my problem, but whoa. While we were talking and wrapping up – the three of them standing about six feet across from me – crash, boom! Two framed pictures from an alcove bookshelf a few feet to my left landed close to my feet. *Duder!* The buyer immediately said something like, "Well maybe someone doesn't want me to buy this house" and we all laughed, ha ha ha. I wanted to believe it was him being funny, but the crashing sound was so disarming and made it seem almost violent. I had to know and I had to know then. This was no time for sitting in a circle of candles and invoking our higher selves.

Cue the *Mission: Impossible* music. The door was pretty much hitting them in their asses, "Nice to meet you, enjoy the house!" and I was on the phone with Elizabeth. She just happened to be in my neighborhood, no kidding, and was more than willing to come over right then and there when I told her I just *had* to talk to Duder. Psychic 911, house call edition. Gotta love that. She was there not ten minutes later, we sat down on the couch and pretty much got right to it and, uh oh, there was a very strange look on her face. It was full of question marks and upset and because I know her so well, I knew that she didn't want me to know what she was seeing. *Oh God.* On this particular occasion at this particular moment, her abilities always being far more than what I know about, she actually went to him instead of dialing him up to come to us. I didn't quite realize that at the time, but clarified it with her later.

Okay. So you know how when you open a door to a room and you see something you did *not* want to see and you immediately shut the door wishing you hadn't seen it? Or how when you open a door to a room and you see something you did *not* want to see and you just stand there and keep looking at it? Elizabeth chose option two and all I could do was watch her face while she was watching something I had no idea about. "What?! *What?!*" She was telling me that we (*we?!*) had interrupted Duder while he was reviewing some of his actions in a previous life. (He had told me in the New Year's Eve conversation that the reviewing of life was an ongoing process. Apparently it was the reviewing of *lives* that was ongoing). Elizabeth appeared on the scene when he was needing to face something that was very difficult for him to face and which upset him very much, the repercussions of actions he had taken in that life, whenever that was. He was accompanied not by the guides who had been with him before, but by two different ones who Elizabeth took an immediate dislike to. She didn't like the tone and task-master-like manner they were taking with him and she felt like they were forcing him to do something he didn't want to be doing because of how upset he clearly was. She was instantly emotionally involved, bless her heart, and so protective. And here I am, psychic hotline emergency, wanting to know if it was him who knocked the pictures off the shelves. *Awkward.* (For the record, he later said that, yes, it was a very upsetting experience but there was nothing forced about it.)

Everybody and everything settled down. Duder was free to come and talk with us, however that happened, and when he did he came with these same two other guides, the ones Elizabeth was not liking. The good news was he was here and could hang out; the bad news was that they – all three of them – were asking Elizabeth to channel, to allow Duder to speak *through* her, no charades necessary. Sidebar: That, in itself, was fascinating because she had never channeled before. But she had, at the new year, asked to expand her work, to be able to reach more people, and for opportunities to be of greater service. Ya just gotta be careful about whatchya ask for! Here was an opportunity for her to "be of greater service," not very long into the new year, but no way. Not that day. She didn't like those other beings, she didn't trust them and, besides, channeling Duder, she told me later, felt almost incestuous. So we would do this the old fashioned way.

Yay. Time for my super important question and, yes, it was him. All three times. The magnet, the Christmas ornament, and the picture frames. And, oh yes, of course, it was about the old *everything is energy* concept. He was able to move the magnet and then move the Christmas ornament at my friend's homes because there was just more energy in those places to work with. In particular, my friend with the ornament is a frenetic guy who lives in a frenetic house with CNN on *all* day (for his dog, don't get me started) and the energy there is a-swirling. Always. My house? Not so much. It was still ultra-peaceful and calm, extremely, which certainly served its purpose for Duder as he was departing this plane and for me, in general, because I like it that way. But it's not a lot to go on if you're a non-physical being looking to stir up some trouble. When the new owner and his cohorts showed up, Duder hit pay dirt and let me have it. Emergency over and out.

∞

In another brief, unscheduled conversation shortly before I moved, Duder said he was sad that "we" were leaving the beach because he really loved it there: the house, the town, the beach itself, and the life we had only just begun to share there. But he understood and was fully supportive and thought the energy in the mountain house was strong and good. "What's that?," I asked. Elizabeth had been downloading a story or something. He was saying he helped me get the house. Those three days of silence? He kind of helped to delay the realtor from calling me to tell me the owners were moving on. He showed Elizabeth the office where the realtor worked and also who she was. Elizabeth's description of it and her was right on the money. It amused and comforted me to know that not only did he know the house I would be moving in to, he actually helped me to get it. And, oh yes, he was coming with me.

Solitude, Cheating, and A Big Insight
March 1, 2006 – June 24, 2006

In the course of a few hours my transplant to the mountains was complete and I noticed I wasn't looking back even for a moment. I remember saying to people at the time that I felt as though, when all was said and done, after 20 years, I'd lived at the beach for the exact perfect number of minutes I was supposed to. I'd gone from living at sea level to living 5,400 feet above it, from palm trees to pine trees, from an ocean view to a mountain view, from beach to forest, from west-facing sunsets to east-facing sunrises, from rollerblading to hiking, from having a partner to not, and so much more. The move itself couldn't have been simpler and smoother and it felt so right, a hundred percent. I was welcomed in my first days by back-to-back storms which, combined, dumped about a foot and a half of snow, novelty upon novelty. On my third or fourth day, surrounded on the inside by unpacked boxes and on the outside by white as far as the eye could see, with the wood burning stove cranking at full blast and a silence that enveloped everything, I stared out at my new environs for hours and it never got boring. I was, indeed, home.

If you told me you found sanctuary in your home and loved it beyond measure and felt more than lucky to have it, there's a fairly good chance I'd launch into a screed about how there's no such thing as luck because *everything is energy* vibrating at one level or another and how our world, hardly a secret, is based on the *law of attraction* and how there are no accidents and that just as we must *take responsibility* for the things we've attracted into our lives that we deem to be undesirable, we must also *take responsibility* for the things we've attracted into our lives we deem to be desirable. I'd cajole you to take notice of and credit for what you'd created for yourself if not entirely by yourself. Duder? He'd just tell you to take a bow. I laughed when I thought about that and figured I should probably do as he or I would probably suggest. So I acknowledged that I had created for myself a stunning place to live and, simultaneously, because nothing comes from nothing, I expressed heartfelt *gratitude* to Source for its part in this particularly magnificent co-creation.

I was in a wonderfully healing place, no doubt about it, and healing – processing through the layers of what it was like to be living without Duder and what it was like to have helped him leave his body – was the first and pretty much only order of business. The move had afforded me something of a time and money cushion and I was taking full advantage of it. I had also decided that starting a new chapter of life would be the perfect time for a cleanse – you know, drinking juice and not eating food for a while to detoxify and all that? Duder thought so too, bless his little heart. When he was here, he twice did them with me and while he was definitely into the idea, it was all new to him and he very much followed my lead. Now, over there, my new spiritual teacher/guide/angel/brother/friend was all about it, telling me in that last session with Elizabeth "It will raise your vibration" and "will help with our communication." And he was serious! This bit about his in-depth knowledge of numberless topics was still taking some getting used to and I continued doing audio double-takes whenever I heard any of it.

Between the snow, my buried car, and a lack of need for groceries, I pretty much spent my first two weeks in the mountains "alone," settling into my new house, meditating in the morning with my new spirit guide and, most evenings, having spiritual hour 2.0 with Duder and the circle and the candles – an energetic field of us. *Holy us.* I loved the idea of reserving the time and creating the space to share together. And it was fun discovering that I could beckon him at any time by either talking to him in my mind, out loud, or some combination of the two and *feeling* him appear on the spot. The clear distinction between the tinglies and *his* tinglies was now firmly established and it was so comforting to know that he was always quite close.

I didn't have any real expectations for our new spiritual hours, I'd learned about that a long time ago. But I will cop to a bit of wishin' and a-hopin' that something huge would happen, that I'd see him like Elizabeth did or even hear him or levitate from the sheer force of our energetic field or something, but no such nothing. It became an opportunity, however, to see very clearly how *judgments separate us* because if we were creating an energetic field of us with the *intent* of enhancing our communication and I sat in it without any attachment to how it should be and simply let it be how it was, then I stayed connected. The moment I called it something like stupid or a waste of time or embarrassing (have to admit it), I felt an immediate separation from the experience and from him, the opposite of what I was looking for. Duly noted.

∞

The big Duder cries found me in the mountains, no surprise. I took note of an uptick in their frequency, which I attributed – not that it mattered, really – to a marked decrease in my own daily activity as well as the sinking in of it all, the *reality*. So I did what I encourage anyone else to do when emotions come calling: let them in, don't *judge* them, and let them through. Nothing new here. A typical big cry lasted ten or fifteen minutes, sometimes less, sometimes more, and it was becoming clear that they were, for sure, part of my processing experience, but just a part of it; a nice place to visit, perhaps even necessary, but I wouldn't want to live there and I didn't – and I was beginning to understand why.

My big cry process at the time went pretty much like this: Step one, feel the feeling whenever it shows up (or as soon as possible thereafter), preferably without *judgment*. Got it. (And take a Duder bow for *being present*.) Step two, optional, look for the thoughts that connect to the feeling. *He's not here.* True. *He's not coming back.* True. *I can't touch him.* True. Reasonable thought-to-feeling, feeling-to-thought ratio and also a good execution of *being present*, so far. Step three, paradox, realize that while *being present* means to let in the feelings when they come, it also means not to dwell on the thoughts connected to the feelings because dwelling on those thoughts – *he's not here,* etc. – would require thinking about what was not and what would never be, a violation of *being present* if ever there was one. Tricky, perhaps, but not impossible.

And then I noticed how virtually any other thought I could possibly have about the whole thing was also a thought that would take me out of *being present*. "This isn't fair" was a dead-ender because it implied that his being alive – not an option – *would* be fair. Ten *being present* demerits. "We were ripped off" implied that something had gone terribly wrong, which defied the concept that *we are here for a reason*, in whatever present moment we're ever in, and that there are no accidents. "What a tragedy," same thing. "We were supposed to have been together for decades," same thing. "This really sucks," nothing more than a *judgment* that separated me from the experience. It was like I would have the thought and as I was having it, it would practically dissolve on the spot because I didn't really *believe* it and therefore couldn't and didn't invest it with any real energy. (Sorry, conventional wisdom.)

And what crystallized for me was an ancient teaching I learned in a contemporary way a couple of decades earlier: pain is inevitable, misery is optional. Bingo! I could actually *feel* how if I held on to any one of "those thoughts," I would create unending sorrow and/or suffering and/or misery and/or oh yes, there it was, drumroll please...grief. A-*ha*! Identifying with "It's not fair" and "We should have been together for decades" and "thoughts like those" would absolutely produce grief because they kept me out of the *present*. I wasn't experiencing grief because I wasn't entertaining the range of non-present-moment thoughts that create it!

Now my motivation for not entertaining "those thoughts" was rooted in my *intention* simply to live my life the best I could in the present moment, an *intention* I'd set a long time before all this. On that level it had nothing to do with Duder being gone and everything to do with living a spiritually responsible life. Still, it often seemed mighty tempting to really lose myself in them once in a while, in "This isn't fair" and "We were ripped off" and "I don't want to live without you" because all the emotion – the grief, really – kind of kept me connected to him in much the same way that I felt connected during a big Duder cry. But the reality of it was when I let go of all that and, in a very real sense, let go of him in the process, I actually got more of him in the *present* moment. By not indulging thoughts of what wasn't, I was open to what was. Again. And what was, was that he was here, with me, loving me, teaching me, tingling me, challenging me to grow, to evolve, to become even more of who I was. There was no getting around it.

∞

At the end of March, I decided to avail myself of a reading with a different medium. She had been highly recommended by two friends who, without much or any experience with this sort of thing, had each had sessions with her that blew them away. Of course, I was already quite used to being blown away during sessions with mediums so I took on a very laissez faire, we'll-just-see-about-that attitude when I decided to cheat on Elizabeth. Well I guess it's not really cheating if you tell the other person, which I did and she was eager to hear all about it.

Usually when I schedule a reading, I know ahead of time who I want to talk to and what I want to talk about. Sometimes it goes exactly as planned and often it goes into all different directions, either because they bring up different topics or because entities I hadn't counted on show up and are eager to contribute their own input. This time I was leaving it completely open. I wasn't requesting that my new guide come and talk to me; I wasn't requesting that my grandmother and great aunts come and talk to me; I wasn't requesting that Duder come and talk to me. I was really and truly leaving it wide open, essentially saying to any non-physical being of light and love that may have been hanging around me at the time to please come forward with anything they felt I needed to know, if there was anything. My *intention* was simply to *be present* and to see what would arise.

I liked this 40-ish woman right off the bat. She had an energy I connected with and I was excited by the prospects of the session. While Elizabeth mainly sees, this medium told me that she sees *and* senses (feels) *and* hears and not to worry about it. Fair enough. We got underway and the first five or ten minutes were kind of rocky. She was definitely tuning in to a particular energy, but couldn't conjure a good description, at least of anyone that seemed recognizable to me. Then there was a shift of sorts and I thought she said that whoever had been there was now stepping aside or leaving and a different being was coming in. Then she said something about red hair – Duder! – and to my great joy, it was him. Unmistakably. I could feel him, too.

This reading actually lasted about two and a half hours and I wish I had that much time's worth of details to share with you, but I don't. It just kind of whizzed by, though the feelings I had afterward lasted and still linger. Right off the bat, he made a point of telling the medium to tell me that he was there by himself, no brother, and I felt so loved in that moment. It was striking to me that he could know something that would make me happy – even if I never expressed it with words – and that he simply chose to do it. Just like when he was here, just like what people in love do for one another.

Now it's hard to tell you about this without sounding like some kind of egomaniac because Duder was using this medium, it seemed to me, like she'd been a friend of his or something. He was talking to her as if I wasn't there while she, of course, had to tell me what he was saying. He started talking to her about how incredibly wonderful it was to have been loved by me. In no time he was pouring it on – thick. "He's telling me that you would deny it, but that you'd have given him your heart, literally, if he needed it," she said. "He's telling me that you loved wholly and completely. He's telling me about how much he enjoyed your sex life and how he regrets that you didn't have more time together for that." He was making her laugh as he went on and on about how breathtakingly magnificent I was and it was obvious that he liked her, too. It was like he was bragging to her about his having been with such an astonishingly brilliant and multi-faceted man. (Have I made my point?) Then something happened which caught me off guard. She stopped the reading in its tracks with, "Hold on just a moment..." and looked at me and asked, dead serious, "Do you have a brother?!" Feeling like I'd been whooping it up on an amusement park ride that came to a sudden and screeching halt I said, "Excuse me?" She was talking to us – both of us – like we were old friends when she said she was divorced, single, and looking for a new relationship – and she was looking for exactly what Duder was describing to her about me and what she was experiencing about us. Thank you very much.

We chatted a bit more about her and when we continued, with her actually being a medium again, the compliments from Duder kept on coming. That he was essentially telling her romantic, loving, couple-y stuff, in front of me, so to speak, with her having to relay it all to me, added a healthy measure of hilarity to the session. She said some more to me about, really, did I have a brother, and what did she need to do to find love like ours? Then she howled with laughter and told me that Duder was telling her that there would be no new man in her future until she did something with her hair. I wish I was kidding. But he knew that *she* wanted and/or needed a hair makeover (it looked fine to me) and she certainly took whatever Duder said in the "spirit" in which it had been intended, agreeing with him wholeheartedly. Classic Duder. He was having fun with her, I was having fun being showered in his love and compliments, and, if possible, she was having more fun than either of us.

Duder and I had always been very communicative about how we felt about one another and about our relationship. It was never in doubt. But three months after he'd left I have to admit I had begun to question and wonder a little. Because he had "died," was I building him up in my mind? Was I making more of our relationship than it was? Was I exaggerating my feelings for him or his for me? Survey says? Absolutely not! And what a tremendous gift it was to receive this communication from him when this uncharacteristic vulnerability on my part was bubbling below the surface.

Our new friend interrupted him again, looked at me directly, as her, and said she just had to tell me/us what a joy it was to be with us right now. She added that so often in her readings there are people with so much unresolved business and she often witnesses much anger and contempt and hostility. It was clear that she was not just witnessing our love, but experiencing it herself. (Elizabeth has said the same thing.) She looked right at me and said, "Wow. You guys really had something" and I said, "Had?"

Then there was an odd moment where it seemed like they were talking amongst themselves and she was slacking on the sharing it with me part. She kind of smiled, knowingly, and looked at me with a hint of trepidation as she relayed Duder's message. He said, first and foremost, that he knew it was really far too soon to be talking about what was coming, but he had to tell me because it had come up in the ethers somehow and to ignore it would violate some truth code over there or something. Then he said that a full and loving relationship would absolutely be part of my experience again in this life and he was right. It was far too soon to be talking about it.

Only three months after he'd left, the singular conscious thought I'd had about another relationship – prompted by having been asked about it – was an intellectual, law of averages thought or acknowledgment that many people in my position find themselves in wonderful relationships again. But there was absolutely no way I could connect to the concept on an emotional level and I certainly wasn't trying to. It was like, yeah, I suppose that can or will happen one day, but I have no idea how and I really don't care. The topic occupied something like a fraction of a fraction of a piece of a percentage point of my time and energy. Or less. And I wasn't looking to increase it, not by a long shot.

Could we get back to the lovefest, please?! We had gone way beyond our scheduled time, but I sought to clear up what was, for me, the only scrap of unfinished Duder business I had and everyone was game. It was about that conversation we'd started back in Mexico when I gave him those clinical-sounding answers to his questions about whether or not I had cried about any of what had been happening that year. I told him how bad I felt about my response and that I was a little concerned he might have taken it as not caring. *And how cool was it that I could clear the air like this? And why didn't everyone?* He said he understood completely what I was saying back in Mexico and what I was saying in this session, that I couldn't possibly have imagined what it would be like to not have him physically in my life or that it would produce such feelings of emptiness, loss, and sadness. How does one imagine that? He said he knew all about the big Duder cries and how much I loved him and that's what he was giving back to me right there, in that session with a "translator" we'd never met: a big, giant dose of "I love you that much, too." Thanks, Duder.

∞

That reading left me blissfully saturated with all kinds of Duder love which, in turn, humbled me all over again, produced new insights, and advanced me in my process. I became even more aware of the *choice* I had between focusing on the very real loss and emptiness and sadness or the truly real love we were, quite obviously, still sharing. I was aware of the *choice* before but now it seemed more stark, more clear. His physicality was gone, but our love for one another and the deep connection we enjoyed was still ever-present and that was made obvious in the session we'd just had. Love was continuing to flow between us, love that was full to overflowing, love that was expanding, love that another could get caught up in. Making the *choice* to focus on that love instead of the body it used to come through and re-making and re-making and re-making that *choice* – sometimes many times a day – was a considerable part of why the big Duder cries didn't take me down, down, down when they beckoned. And why grief stayed away.

But there was something else that dawned on me after that session which helped me to navigate through life without my partner more than any other single element in my entire process. It was a thought, really, an obvious extension of all that *being present* thinking. It occurred to me that if I *believed* (and I did) that Duder was where he was supposed to be and that it was not an accident and *for a reason,* then the corollary of that – what I was also compelled to *believe* – was *I am supposed to be here without him.* Holy crap! *I am supposed to be here without him.* I could feel at once how the *energy* of that thought differed from the *energy* of those "other thoughts." *I am supposed to be here without him.* That was my spiritually responsible higher self talking, not the human egoic part that wanted him right here with me the way it was *supposed* to be. And there it was: *He's supposed to be here with me* vs. *I am supposed to be here without him.* Thinking the first one produced sadness; thinking the second one produced wonder; *believing* the first one by thinking it over and over again would have produced grief/misery/suffering; *believing* the second one produced even more wonder so I *believed* it and I wondered.

If I was supposed to be here without him, that meant there was more in store for me in this life; if there was more in store for me in this life, I'd want to bring my full self to it; in order to bring my full self to the rest of my life, I would need to honor the process I was in and experience it fully; in order to honor it and experience it fully, I needed to give it its due; in order to give it its due, I had to do what I was doing. Alrighty then.

And if I was supposed to be here without him, I was not supposed to be partnered with him for the rest of my life;

if I was not supposed to be partnered with him for the rest of my life, I might *choose* (and you-know-who said I would) to be partnered with someone else; if I would someday be partnered with someone else, I'd want to bring my full self to that relationship; in order to bring my full self to another relationship, I would need to honor this process and experience it fully. 'Round and 'round we go.

And if I was supposed to be here without him, there was no sense bemoaning the fact that I was here without him (oh that again); when I did not bemoan the fact that I was here without him, I could ponder the possibilities; when I pondered the possibilities I felt free and unencumbered; when I felt free and unencumbered, it made me miss him even more; when I missed him, I realized that he was still here; when I realized he was still here, I remembered I could still talk with him; when I talked with him, I felt comforted and supported; when I felt comforted and supported, I could again ponder the possibilities of why it was I was now here without him. One might say I was on a bit of a roll.

Now I have seen in my own experience and in the experiences of many people with whom I work that even when we accept that there are no accidents, that we are never in the wrong place, and that it's all *for a reason*, we still often wonder what the hell the reason is. I had learned a long time ago (from Rev. Dr. Michael Beckwith) that a good question to ask in these situations is, What muscle(s) do I need to grow or develop or strengthen in order to navigate through this circumstance? (Or, What am I being challenged to do? or Who am I being challenged to be?) On a higher self level, there will always be something custom-made for our learning and enlightenment. Having landed on the whole *I am supposed to be here without him* notion, I could see right away that at least one of the reasons my higher self had directed me to this place was so I could strengthen my faith. Yes, that. I was being asked to trust All That Is that my highest good was being served by living here without Duder, without the perfect partner, without the laughter, without, without. I knew deep down that investing some time and energy in the Trust God department was spot on for me and it was remarkable to *feel* the peace created by that thought.

As you can see, *believing* I was supposed to be here without him changed the entire trajectory of my process and inspired me, among other things, to reconsider the story Duder and I had created about ourselves when we came together. You know, the one about how we would *be* together – in physical form as romantic partners – for decades to come? Ha! That one emanated from our human selves and, obviously, there was far more to it. So I began to think about a more metaphysically-based story about our souls, which began when we were in whatever space we occupy before we incarnate. Then I realized that starting there was entirely arbitrary and thought about a more appropriate place to begin. A few centuries ago? A thousand lifetimes ago? The first time we met as spirits? And where would it end? Creating this new story was going nowhere and I realized it was probably because grasping the true breadth and depth of my connection to and love for and history with Duder was probably in the incomprehensible category. Inquisitive as I can be about all things metaphysical, I was oddly content knowing what he had already told me, that our relationship spanned myriad lifetimes. I was equally content knowing that whatever our two years together here as a couple were about, they were but a tiny speck in the greater story of who we are to each other. And as I write our story with his constant presence, support, and assistance, I feel sure that it is just one of a number of projects we have collaborated on and that many more will follow. That's enough for me and already a way different – and a way larger – story than the one our human selves whipped up soon after we found each other and became Duders.

∞

Knowing and trusting that I was supposed to be here without him also motivated me to consider something I'd always wanted to do which just wasn't practical when I lived at the beach: throw an annual party to celebrate summer, my favorite season. My new, far more remote location would require some advance planning for any friends who would want to come so if I was going to do it, I'd have to decide pretty soon and get the word out. I deliberated with my conscience about the appropriateness of it all, given that the party would be only six months after Duder's departure, calendar stuff I really didn't care to indulge for its own sake; I deliberated with my heritage which teaches that celebrations of any kind should not be engaged in until 11 months after the death of a spouse or immediate relative (calendar stuff ala the Jews); and I deliberated with Duder who said to go for it so I sent out the invitations. (Sorry, Jews; sorry calendar).

Spring came into full bloom and as I continued to think and feel my way through this whole being here without him thing, it got mildly confusing because he was still here with me so much of the time. I was getting more and more confident in my ability to discern his presence, even as I knew (because he told me) that sometimes I didn't. He also told me that if he wasn't around and I wanted to talk to him, he could always "pick up messages." (These ditties were part of the last conversation we'd had through Elizabeth.) So I would say things to him all the time and not worry for a moment about whether or not he knew that I was talking to him. I was also working hard to tread beyond feeling his presence into picking up on what he might be trying to say to me, but I can't say I had much success with that.

At the end of April I took what would be my last consulting job. I'd been inching toward this point in my career for a long time, the point where I left behind all the old safety nets and devoted time only to what it was I wanted to do: spirituality work. The consulting project was particularly awful and for about two-and-a-half or three weeks I allowed myself to be yanked out of my processing space and back into the corporate abyss – not quite an energetic match for where I'd been. The project ended on a Friday and the following Monday, in early May, I returned to writing the book I had been fully committed to writing not long before Duder was diagnosed. Energy re-aligned. I'd put it to the side when it was clear he was going to leave and now, six months later, when I picked it up again, Duder flooded me with tinglies again and again. Of course. Nobody was more supportive of my fledgling writing career than he was and he never wanted me to get de-railed from it because of his illness. (He never mentioned anything about getting de-railed from it because of his "death.") His encouragement and enthusiasm were invaluable when he was here in his body and they were invaluable when he was here without his body.

Resuming the writing routine I'd established a year and a half earlier was a snap and I loved it. I would spend from about 7:30 or 8:00 in the morning until about 1:00 or 2:00 in the afternoon at the computer and then had the rest of my days, as my guide had suggested, simply to be. I had dialed back on spiritual hour 2.0 with Duder, favoring a more relaxed, spontaneous manner of communication, delighting in feeling his presence, talking to him, leaving him messages, crying the big Duder cries when they came, and continuing my life here without him, as it was supposed to be. I ventured out a bit more into my new community, but not too much.

In June, a week or two before the party, I noticed a marked decline in his presence. He was still around, for sure, but noticeably less. This gave me pause until I realized how much sense it made because of how it correlated to the change or evolution in my own thinking and *believing*. The more I thought that I was supposed to be here without him, the more I experienced being here without him. It was another layer of separation and another moment I could point to in the progress of my process.

It was a joy to welcome and be surrounded by my friends and to have the party. I had the sense that most of them were there, at least in part, to check in on me, to see how I was doing in the wake of Duder's absence, and to check out exactly where the heck it was I was living. At that time, I was still unreservedly connected to Duder and found great pleasure in talking about him with anybody who would listen. I was still crying some big Duder cries and was learning so much about us, love, life, and "death." I had said goodbye to my marketing career (after 25 years) and was writing full time. I was shifting from accepting living without him to embracing it. So six months after the telepathic sunset, I think my friends could see I was "doing well."

Help with the Mother of all Issues
June 25, 2006 – September 13, 2006

Summer began to hum along in a way that was custom-made for me. The happy rhythm and flow of writing I had reclaimed was going strong and became the foundation for everything else. The weather was perfect. The creek was running. The house was home. I wasn't a complete hermit, but I was still enjoying copious amounts of time on my own for the Duder processing project. Six months out and then some, what I noticed the most – and not necessarily to my liking – was how much, how often, and how frequently that process changed.

Ah, change. For me it relates to the concept *we belong to the planet, not the planet to us* because if we believe we are really part of the planet, connected to it, made of the same stuff, then to mirror its ways is to mirror well being and one of its ways is change. Constant, never-ending change. So when we accept change on its terms, when we offer no resistance, we are in alignment with the planet and well being – and oh so *present*. So I guess what I'm saying is that when I notice things are changing – perhaps faster than I would have them change – like with Duder – what motivates me to go with the flow of it is the notion that the act of allowing change is, itself, a spiritual pursuit. I'm sorry? That merriment and raucous laughter you're hearing? Oh that's just a chorus of my former and current non-physical guides and teachers and angels and, yeah, sure, probably God, too, who have witnessed me resisting change in such a multitude of ways for, um, a few decades or more. Don't mind them. So my process with Duder was changing and that was okay because it's the nature of the living, breathing planet to change and, therefore, it's the nature of me to change. Got it. At that point it was no longer a frenetic pursuit — *Is that him? Was that drawer open before? Did the light just flicker? What's he trying to say? How about now?* — but rather, more of a dance. I was still strongly guided by the notion that I was supposed to be here without him and he was still hanging around far less than he was during the first five months or so. I wasn't having any conversations with him through Elizabeth or anyone else, but that didn't stop me from thinking about him virtually every minute of every hour of every day. In that way, he was still with me all the time. *All* the time. And, yet, he wasn't.

As summer rolled along, as I got more and more used to the Duder here/not here/here/not here dynamic, as I soaked up mountain living, as my writing progressed, as the big Duder cries waned in frequency, as I reveled in the easy current of this chapter of my life, my mom informed me she needed to have her hip replaced. Oh shit! She and I are the only ones in the family that don't live on the east coast (my dad made his transition a year before Duder did) and she's two hours from me here in California. And we don't have the best of relationships. One word: buzzkill.

A pre-surgery meeting at the factory uh, hospital, with others who would be going through the same thing laid out the pending needs in a straightforward manner: a three-day hospital stay, a 10-day rehab stay, and about two weeks at home with physical therapy before she could go up and down stairs and generally return to normal life. I did the easy math and realized that in order to fulfill my own personal *intentions* to be of service and to exercise a base level of *compassion* by providing assurance to my mom that she would not have to fend for herself during this process, I would pretty much need to be there for a month. Yikes. So I began my attempt to convey to her that I basically had her back. I would live at her place for a month, write while there, and generally be on hand, present, for whatever might be needed. I was happy to do it (okay, *willing*), could do it and, after all, isn't this the reason to have family nearby? If my mother had functioning ears and an ability to see the world as a generally *compassionate* place, we'd be off and running and enjoying the rest of our lunch. But she doesn't.

In fact, there is an industrial strength shredder where her ears should be. It sucks up words, thoughts, and ideas, pulverizes them, and spits them out almost as fast as they go in, in the form of an energetic mass, indistinguishable from anything I'd said or meant to convey, which then begins to fill the space between us until it is so pervasive it crushes life with its weight. On my best days, I can practice a sort of spiritual jiu jitsu and neutralize some of the energy; on my super best days — I think I had one once — I can do so without entirely exhausting myself in the process; on my worst days, the mass just fills the space and I'm done for. So there's that, and there's also her super-human powers of negativity including an ability to resist and/or say no to everything and anything. Automatically. Ever and always. A matter of policy. So the mere offer of what to me is standard compassionate action — *You won't be alone. I'll help with whatever comes up. This is what people do.* – becomes an argument and debate. That's mostly because, bless her heart, she's not a terribly compassionate person and doesn't really understand it or recognize it when it's offered to her. If you can imagine pulling the Titanic up Mt. Everest then you can imagine the effort it takes for me to converse with my mother.

When Duder was here, he was a genius at navigating between us and our historically, forever, wearisome relationship. He provided a terrific buffer and was often able to transmute a good chunk of the pulverized mass while simultaneously helping me – when I could be helped – to see things from her perspective. He also conceded that, yes, she could be a handful and I wasn't entirely crazy. A little of that, let me tell you, went a long, long way.

As departure day approached, thoughts, feelings, and actions unbecoming a spiritually responsible practitioner began to surface. Well, actually, I should re-phrase that so excuse me while I lumber onto my soap box for this sidebar. As far as I'm concerned, being spiritually responsible does not mean never being in a bad mood, having an impure thought, or an overwhelming desire to throttle someone. To have and to experience our emotions is to practice *being present*, accepting them, not resisting them. Being spiritually responsible is about what we *do* with any and all of that stuff when it arises. What I typically do with it – and what I *chose* to do with this particular patch of bad mood, impure thoughts, and overwhelming desire to throttle someone – was to honker down with the 15 concepts with which I work, *intending* an attitude adjustment.

I guess I started with *taking responsibility* which, as a concept, encompasses and connects to a range of thoughts. It reminds me that things don't happen *to* me, but *for* me. I am not a victim but rather the architect of my experiences. I am *here for a reason*, in this moment, with a mother not to my liking, for example, on purpose, for a purpose. No accidents. Never in the wrong place. Then the old, well if that's true, what muscle do I need to grow or develop or strengthen in order to navigate peacefully through this situation? Ooh, ooh, I know! Compassion? But God, really, aren't I a pretty compassionate guy already? Don't I show it with people all the time? Okay, lots of the time? *Yes, but not so much with her.* So that's it? This whole thing is for me to develop my *compassion* muscle? *Is there a clearer way to peace?* Not that I can see. But this is sooooo hard. And monumentally inconvenient. Couldn't we do this some other time? In some other way? *This will serve your highest good.* Because it's here and now, right? *Have faith; trust.* Oh, brother.

Continuing on...review *intentions?* Check. I *intend* to live from my heart and to practice *compassion.* I *intend* to convey to my mother that she is not alone. Be conscious of *choices* being made? Check. I don't have to do any of this; I *choose* to do it. *Be present?* Check. Accept the interruption of writing, again; accept that you're feeling pissed off and bummed out that after all the years and all the forward progress that Working On Your Relationship With Your Mother has produced, you're still capable of generating such powerful, unpleasant emotion. And know that right there is at least one reason why she's in your life: so you can grow that *compassion* muscle big and strong and maybe ixnay on the eactionsray by the time you're 50. (That again.) Continuing on...*beliefs matter?* Check. I *believe* this is the right thing to do. I *believe* there are no accidents and that I am *here* (in this moment) *for a reason.* *Have an attitude of gratitude?* Check with me later. All of this helped to take the edge off, as it always does, but I was not all the way there. No, sir.

Two days or so before my humming summer would grind to a standstill I was still resisting, stomping around like a toddler and, yes, even throwing a couple of choice objects across the room. With velocity. It was a big resistance party and through it all I detected a bit of Duder hanging around. Then the day before I left, while packing up some boxes and still feeling pretty snarky, I felt some more of Duder. Interesting, great. And on the morning I left, as I was packing up the car, still raging against the machine and observing myself in every disheartening moment of it, even more Duder. That's when I realized that after six or more weeks of little or no presence, he'd actually been hanging around for a few days.

"Oh my God! You're here to help me with my mom! Aren't you?! Aren't you?!" And with that, the tinglies – replete with his special accent – flooded me, an acknowledgment that what I'd just said/thought was "true." Knowing he was there and offering support or watching over me or whatever he was doing was all I needed for the stomping and bad attitude to give way to relief and joy. Actual joy. I was heading into the morass, but I had a very special escort which changed the tenor of the entire adventure. *Thanks, Duder, from the bottom of my heart.* He accompanied me for the duration of the two-hour drive and it was wonderful to be sharing time and space with him again. Being with him raised my vibration such that I arrived at my mother's in as good a state of mind as I think was possible for me to attain, especially considering all the resistance I was still feeling and experiencing when it was time to go. I felt so loved and I wasn't resisting anymore. Thirty days, ready or not.

I stayed at my mom's that evening and while that may sound pretty normal to you, the fact is I had never done it before; we're not that kind of mother and son. I took her to the hospital first thing the next morning for her surgery and everything pretty much went as expected until the third day. As she was about to be moved to the nursing home for rehabilitation, something wasn't quite right and they discovered they had screwed up her surgery, fractured her femur, and had to do it again, don't get me started. So three days in the hospital became six. It's typically all I can do to hold on to my soul inside of hospitals and I'd had my share of days spent in those energy sappers in the last two years (my dad and Duder). But oh yeah, this wasn't about me.

Surgery the sequel came and went and by the time my mother was transferred to rehab, I had lived seven days in her apartment, a place full to overflowing with dense energy and virtually devoid of physical comfort, kind of like the hospital. (You and most anyone else would, I'm sure, find it a perfectly lovely place.) Not surprisingly, I wasn't getting any work done which meant my tether to sanity was temporarily unavailable and I hadn't yet sourced another one. From my mother there were oft-repeated complaints of the food – reasonable enough – followed by my oft-repeated offers to bring whatever she wanted – "You can literally have whatever you want" – followed by her oft-repeated refusals. Then, "Oh, you didn't have to do that" as she surveyed, wide-eyed, the hot pastrami sandwich or chocolate donuts or whatever it was I'd brought. "You really didn't have to do that." "Oh that's too much." "You really have to stop doing this." Chomp, chomp. You're welcome. Kill me now.

When nurses and therapists would compliment her about how nice it was that I was so present and keeping up to date on her condition — *isn't this what people do?* — she offered typically snide responses like urging them to find out from me what I did for a living because she, of course, had no idea. "Maybe he'll tell *you*." There were her obsessions with the mail (ninety-nine percent junk), her keys (not much use for them now), phone messages (there are never any phone messages) and other minutiae about which she demanded we converse again and again. (Exactly like always.) The oppressive and relentless heat made its own unique contribution to that week and, of course, there was her shredding machine — turbo-charged by pain medication and some disorientation, poor thing — now eating up any and all medical information pertinent to her condition. The cherry on top was her virtual denial that she'd even had a second surgery and her admonishing me repeatedly not to say anything to anyone, ever, about the doctor's blatant malpractice. "Shhh, I may have to come to this hospital again someday." Fine, her life. And mine? Seven days, of vapid, insipid, non-productivity because, from my and only my perspective, she just couldn't take in or allow my being there, couldn't say thank you, couldn't let me do anything I was there to do, couldn't go with the flow. Relentless, gargantuan resistance just like, uh, who was that again? Me? Oh, mother.

It was late afternoon and we were getting her settled into her room at the rehab place. I was unpacking her things and putting them where she directed me to, and our usual back-and-forth ensued: her complaints, my offers of relief, her refusals. Then I sensed it, The Edge. Hi there. I could feel it and I could practically see it. I stared at it in my mind and felt it in my being while she kept up with her resistances to my tiny efforts to make her life a little less awful, the entire reason I was there instead of living my perfect life at home. Before I knew it, then while absolutely knowing it, I just lunged for it. The Edge, that is. I didn't care. In a desperate and futile attempt to get through to her, I yelled as one would yell in a library with the librarian in his sight line. But that wasn't enough, so I catapulted myself over it, went beyond The Edge, ripped the baseball cap from my head and hurled it at the door, all the while looking at her and knowing that no amount of histrionics on my part would get me a centimeter closer to getting through to her because getting through to her is not an available option. It was an exhausting state of affairs: me freaking out, her having no idea what I'm freaking out about, me freaking out ten or a hundred or a thousand times more because she has no idea why I'm freaking out. If only her roommate had been in the room.

I ultimately left there feeling lower than low for yelling at a 79-year-old lady sitting helpless in her chair, walker in front of her, in a depressing nursing home, absent a single clue. I needed – and, dare I say, wanted – to *be compassionate* but *compassion* could not co-exist with such anger and bitterness and resentment. Something had to give, I had to give it, and I had to get out of there so I could re-group. It was my first time leaving her, her apartment, the hospital, and/or the nursing home in a week. So Much Work over the course of years and years, and it only took seven days for me to be reduced to a five year old.

∞

My old beach stomping grounds was an hour away and I'd made provisional plans to head up there to stay with some friends overnight if my mom got settled into the rehab place. Now that she had and I'd met the director and her nurses and gotten the lay of the land and the schedule they had for her, I called my friends to let them know I was headed their way. It felt like I was going on vacation. I got on the freeway in the late afternoon – the worst possible time for traffic – but I didn't care because I could certainly use the extra time to cool down and transcend the energy of where I'd been. I was so full of anger and bitterness and resentment and so completely over being that guy who, as a full-grown spiritually responsible adult, still filled up with anger, bitterness, and resentment toward his mother. (At least I did when I had to spend a month with her.)

Duder re-appeared on the scene as I was driving. I can't say I'd felt him all that much since he'd escorted me to my mom's and who could blame him? Maybe he was around and I just couldn't feel him through the density of it all. Anyway, I was, of course, happy to have his presence, but I was also embarrassed at how I'd been feeling and behaving. Fortunately, embarrassment doesn't go very far in the non-physical realm – all that *non-judgment* stuff they're so good at over there. He stayed with me as I bumper-to-bumpered my way up the freeway and though I was grateful, I didn't have a lot to offer him at the time. No friendly conversation or goo-gooing over his being with me, no laughing and kidding around like usual. Not only was I steeped in rage and endeavoring earnestly to let go of it and move far beyond it, I was also feeling so out of sorts, so not myself, so disappointed, and so frustrated.

After about an hour, as I approached my exit, I noticed something stunning. Shocking, really. And magical. Somehow, some way, I was free from the anger and bitterness and resentment. I mean, it was gone. Completely. Lifted off me. I tried to conjure it up, tried to feel those feelings, but I couldn't. I had no connection to them whatsoever, couldn't find them if my life depended on it. And how crazy was that? Going from feeling them so strongly to feeling nothing at all. Zilch. Nada. Duder! He'd conducted some kind of healing right there on the freeway, while I was driving, at least that's what my gut told me. And as simple and clean and swift as that intervention appeared to be is as big and powerful and important as it was — on multiple levels.

The first level was a very practical one. Even though I'm pretty well versed in Working Through My Stuff, I was wondering if I had the fortitude to get it all together before I had to return to the black hole the next day. I was in a bad way and he gave me the gift of a fresh start by clearing the emotional deck for me, allowing me the freedom and space to regroup and, then, to re-engage my mother as if the previous week hadn't happened. I was taken aback by how he basically just did it *for* me. That was a new one.

And there was another layer to the practical side of helping me with my mom. Back during that New Year's Eve reading after Duder faded out, I told you that my grandmother (who you'll remember I never knew in this lifetime) uncharacteristically initiated a conversation with me. "I want to talk to you about your mother." She knew I had been lamenting about having to deal with my mother *at all* — in general — even though in the months leading up to that conversation I was far more occupied with Duder and his transition. That night, my grandmother told me that my mother was not a well woman. "She's not a well woman." "She's not a well woman."

As I reflected on that conversation, which I did a lot, it was by far the most dominant message. She had said it over and over again, I kept hearing it in my mind, but I really didn't get it. I didn't get what she meant by it and I certainly didn't know what to do about it. And, honestly, I really didn't care, I don't think, because it didn't change anything. It didn't change the fact that my mom and I were here together and it seemed to be falling on me to be the person she relied on for just about anything (*we are here for a reason*). Still, my grandmother's words stuck with me. "She's not a well woman." And it wasn't until after the spontaneous freeway healing with Duder that those words started making sense to me. I could see more and more clearly how we got into our loop all the time and why it was so exasperating for me. Duder's intervention cleared a path for me to be able to grasp my grandmother's message – eight months later – and it was an enormous contribution to my ability to find a way to peace with my mother.

And the hits just kept on coming. An entirely different level at which Duder's spontaneous freeway healing affected me was that it knocked me off my decade-long obsession with clairvoyance (what Elizabeth does) and clairaudience (clear hearing) and stimulated my relationship to clairsentience (clear feeling) and claircognizance (clear thinking). No easy feat, to be sure, and I almost missed it. It started when I first noticed I couldn't feel those intense feelings anymore and I asked Duder, "Was that you?! Did you do something?!" If a response came, I didn't perceive it. Yet I did have a knowing, a knowing that whatever I was experiencing was the direct result of his intervention. That gut reaction. And that *was* the response – that knowing. Duh! I didn't see him, he didn't whisper it in my ear, I didn't check with Elizabeth, but I *knew* it. And after that day, I began to understand that that knowing was claircognizance, a thought distinguishable from tens of thousands of others by, among other things, its incisiveness and clarity and, for me anyway, how it connected to a physical feeling in the gut.

Thinking about how I couldn't (yet) see and/or hear beings on the other side of the veil was not going to get me where I wanted to go, I knew that. Learning to receive their communications with feelings and thoughts, it was becoming clear to me, very well might, even though I had no idea how I would possibly accomplish it. So – what a concept – after that freeway healing experience I *chose* to focus on what I did have instead of what I didn't have, the same thing as what I was doing with and about Duder, applied to another aspect of life. It didn't make me clairsentient or claircognizant on the spot, but it got me to look for how all that might work.

On the clairsentient front I began to see how it was about much more than feeling tingly, goose-bumpy sensations. (For the record, nothing I'm saying here should pass as anything remotely close to a primer on any of this. I have never taken a class or read a book about it. This is just me fumbling through.) I also started to take note of the ways in which I used my body – ways that I had never noticed before. I saw that sometimes when describing something or someone, I was actually feeling that person or that thing in my body, and describing what I was feeling. When working with a client who had trouble even taking a full deep breath, I could feel her tension in my body and breathe through it *for* her. *We are all connected.* When holding different thoughts, I would feel them in my body, confirming on a feeling level what I'd received on a thinking level. All in all, I began to learn about ways in which I could use my body to receive communication, perceive information, and direct energy. Baby clairsentient steps inspired by Duder's magic.

On the claircognizant front I really started to take in how frequently, over the course of many years, I'd heard myself say "sometimes I just *know* things." It never seemed particularly meaningful to me before, but I had to admit it happened a lot. So I started working on how it was that I knew things and on deciphering which thoughts were *those* thoughts and I began to see that there was no single way to do that. Certain thoughts would repeat themselves and others would be so succinct and clear that they broke through the thousands of others. Sometimes, when working individually with clients, I would know exactly what the issue was and how to address it, sometimes while they were still uttering their first sentence. I just *knew*. Then there was learning the ways in which thoughts interacted with feelings and I saw how sometimes I would go on feeling alone, sometimes on thought alone, and more and more frequently I experienced how they worked together. And, by the way, it was not lost on me that the telepathic sunset experience right after Duder crossed over was, now that I thought about it, all claircognizance and clairsentience.

So after that day, I relaxed far more into developing my own ways to communicate with the other side and to trust those ways. Ah, trust. Now the effects of the freeway healing rippled even further because *trusting*, in general, is one of the things I am sure I came to learn and develop in this incarnation. *We are here for a reason.* And I was beginning to see how clairsentience and claircognizance would help me with that, too, because as far as I was concerned, they were "harder" than clairvoyance or clairaudience would be. I figured if I woke up one day and saw Duder or my spirit guide lurking at the end of my bed or heard God talking in my ear, well, that would be that. Nothing to trust. But if I had to *feel* them and/or figure out which thoughts they were giving me and which ones were mine all mine, I would have to trust. A whole lot. So for someone who is here at least in part to learn to trust *and* is obsessed with communicating with the other side, perhaps developing clairsentience and claircognizance would be a really good way to go because they seem to demand a level of trust I had not yet mastered. And finally, Duder hadn't been around for a while and then showed up when it was time for me to go to my mom's. When I was in need, he appeared, without my having had to ask for it. So this intervention was another way for me to experience and learn about trust. He'll be there. Someone will be there. Someone is always there. Trust *that*.

∞

On the freeway and in an instant, Duder lightened my energetic load and got me back to center. That spiritual re-boot allowed me to re-engage my mother from a *compassionate* place again and it freed up space for my grandmother's eight-month-old message to permeate my being, rendering me even more *compassionate* with my mom as time went on. The experience of knowing on the spot that he had done something inspired me to develop new ways to *listen to inspiration* and to rely on myself and the ways of our Universe to communicate clearly with the non-physical realm. And he offered up opportunities to strengthen my trust muscle. This is all soul work, work I came here to do, on purpose for a purpose. *(We are here for a reason.)* And here was this being, no longer my physical partner, no longer around me all the time, no longer someone I could touch and share day-to-day lives with, but very much involved in helping me to evolve, grow, and become even more of who I am.

Needless to say, I had some questions. Were there certain "responsibilities" he was taking on with regard to me? Was he stepping in where others might otherwise be? If he hadn't intervened that day, would another entity have? Who? Did it matter? Was I blocking their efforts (like my mom does, mirror mirror on the wall)? Was I able to receive something like that from him because of the special connection we shared? Was his helping me a volunteer mission or part of his work or a project he volunteered for as part of his work? It felt spontaneous, but was it? I certainly asked these and other questions in subsequent sessions, formal and otherwise, with Elizabeth. But they weren't so much answered. Or were they? Because what came to me very clearly, in thought and in feeling, was that sometimes it's best to just stop asking, get out of my head, experience, feel, and be. And trust.

The Defiant Calendar
September 14, 2006 — December 6, 2006

My mother survived her new hip *and* my help and was fending for herself, well enough. I survived my mother and was blissfully on my way back to the mountains, albeit to what seemed like another different life. When I arrived back in town, the first thing I noticed was that autumn had replaced summer, reminding me that, oh yeah, some places actually have seasons and I was living in one of them again. It was late on a Thursday afternoon when I pulled in and before I even went to my house, I stopped at the local organic co-op market to stock up before closing time. The first thing one of the owners said to me — not two minutes after I walked in — was that a particularly large space had become available and did I want it for a healing center? He could show it to me right away.

"Excuse me? Nice to see you, too," I said. "And what the hell are you talking about?" He didn't have much of a response other than to say he thought I might be interested. While I was away, I had put forth a small marketing effort — mostly via him targeted to his clientele — for a "healing event" that Saturday which, apparently, had taken hold. I told him I'd get back to him about his ideas after it was over. The event was really a local version of a project I'd been involved with for a while when I still lived in L.A. No longer operating, its intent was to afford people interested in health and healing the opportunity to get a taste of some different modalities that they may not otherwise have had access to for a very low cost – a simple concept called "community healing." I had invited three of my former colleagues to participate and, beforehand, had introduced them to Elizabeth and the five of us worked as a team seeing about 35 people for 20-25 minute sessions over the course of a day and a half. Some of us also did private sessions on the second day.

Endeavoring to stay ever-present, I hadn't been thinking much beyond putting on that one event. All I did was say to myself (and maybe a few others) that if there was a clamoring for more after we did it, we'd do more. Practically before it got underway, a woman I had never seen, met, or heard of came up to me and asked what I would call a "healing center" if I had one. I thought that was strange, had no answer for her, and didn't yet connect it to the question my friend had asked about a location for such a place two days earlier. Ultimately, those who participated in the event couldn't say enough about what a great experience they had and the clamoring for more, more, more was imposing and impossible to ignore.

Thankfully, the practitioners I'd invited also had good experiences and were willing to come back again so we scheduled another one for mid-November. At the same time, there was an opportunity to strike while the iron was hot so a week after the first event, I began facilitating a class I'd been envisioning for a long time called the Spiritual Workout. As of this writing, it has been running weekly for a year-and-a-half and is still going strong. Separate from any and all of that, I was quite determined to finish writing the proposal for my book and I was still continuing to learn so much about me and

Duder. Life was whizzing along in a manner quite different from what I had grown accustomed to before my month in exile. Now I was involved with projects that included other actual people and the phone calls, emails, meetings, marketing and promotion that went with it. No big deal, just suddenly far busier with more on my plate than I was used to. To be sure, I was missing the kind of time I had been gifted with earlier in the year for the Duder processing project.

∞

After a few weeks at home – in mid-October – I noticed that I had somehow become a blubbering mass of hyper-emotion and I had no idea why. I wasn't crying the big Duder cries – they had largely subsided by then, surprising me once in a while with their sudden onsets but nothing like they had been during the first several months. This was different. It was a far more generalized emotionality which had me choking up and shedding tears at the drop of a hat. Not making an obvious connection between the blubbering and anything that was going on in my life, I basically settled into it and observed it. I knew it would all make sense at some point – and then it did. Despite my determination to not give credence to the calendar, I noticed that, according *to* the calendar, I was cycling back over the period of time when everything started going south with Duder the year before. Fascinating.

In October of the previous year, he wound up having to have surgery to repair a complication from his initial surgery. The complication had dogged him from the get-go, keeping him from strictly following his treatment protocol for weeks at a time, several times, and sometimes – like when he had to be in the hospital for the second surgery – from following it at all. He came through it as well as could have been expected but, still, it seemed to have sapped him of a lot of his physical strength, a lot of his spirit, a lot of his positivity, and a lot of his heart. He didn't feel well, he didn't look well, and this was when I knew he wouldn't survive.

I had to stop in the midst of the emotional helter skelter I'd been living in to laugh at my plan to shun the calendar. My only *intention* was to not make anything out of anniversary dates for the sake of making anything out of anniversary dates. For me, it's all about how *beliefs matter* and if you *believe* it's going to be a difficult day or a difficult time to reflect on what happened a year or five years or ten or a zillion years later then, well, of course it will be. I saw no reason to set myself up for any of that and, to be honest, it's not something I tend to do much of anyway.

But it was as if the calendar had tentacles, or something, that could suck me into its grips despite my plan. I was stunned at its ability to do so but once I was in, once I connected my emotional turbulence to the fact that I was rolling over a pretty intense time from the previous year, and once I let go of my resistance to not listening to the calendar, the dates flooded back to me in rapid succession:

October 21 – Into hospital for tests and prep; his parents arrive

October 25 – Surgery

October 31 – Released from hospital; his parents leave

November 8 – Back to hospital in Mexico

November 20 – Home from Mexico

November 23 – Our anniversary

November 24 – Thanksgiving

November 25 – His birthday; two final nights in the mountains; close up house

December 6 – Call hospice

December 13 – His parents arrive

December 20 – His last day here

I could write paragraphs and paragraphs about each and every one of these days and the periods of time between; they each had their own distinct weight, their own energy, their own remembrances, and their own emotions. And many of them could be placed under the umbrella of Helping Duder Leave the Planet. When it was all happening the previous year, I personally – and apparently – wasn't feeling any of it. I was so involved in caring for him and helping him to leave that I wasn't even aware of how much emotion I wasn't aware of. This is not typical for me, but there it was. And now the Universe, in its compassionate way, was giving me another opportunity to process it all so process it I did, whenever it came. A triumphant performance on American Idol? Boo hoo. A stranger's smile? Boo hoo. The beauty of the trees? Boo hoo. A puppy? You got it.

In fact, I was experiencing something that I'd not only learned a long time ago, but that I remind clients and students of all the time: that when we allow emotion to lie dormant in us, unprocessed, it will look for opportunities to come out. One way or another. People tell me constantly that life doesn't always graciously afford them opportunities to tend to their emotions. They say they can't sit down to identify their feelings and allow them to process through when they're traveling on business and surrounded by co-workers all the time, or when they're sitting in meetings, or when they're juggling the family's schedules, or when they're working 60 hours a week or more or, like in my case, when they're devoted entirely to someone else's needs for a period of time. I get it. But that doesn't change the necessity of doing so if one has *intended* overall spiritual and, yes, physical health. *Choices abound.* I was relieved that it came up for me the way it did because I never would have gone looking for it. I wouldn't have known to.

Another fascinating aspect of this for me was seeing more levels at which *beliefs* operate. I thought I had a *belief* that anniversaries are unimportant. But the emotional flashback to the previous year I was experiencing – on the very anniversary of when it all happened – proved to me that something else was at play. On a conscious level, my *belief* was that anniversaries are whatever one makes them and, like I said, I just wasn't all that interested in making anything out of Duder-related ones, certainly not just for the sake of it. But underneath it all, surprisingly enough, I did align with a *belief* that said something about the power and/or importance of anniversaries or of death anniversaries in particular. People I work with are often amazed to discover how dominant *beliefs* can lie far below the ones they think are dominant. I, too, was amazed to see this in myself.

So I was in this tempest of free-flinging emotion and while I felt as though I had a pretty good handle on the roots of it, I was still kind of surprised that there was so much; it felt rather disproportionate, like I didn't quite have the whole thing yet. And even though I'd been getting better and better at knowing when Duder was around and had been playing for a while with trying to decipher thoughts he might be trying to communicate, my emotional frazzle was impeding my fledgling abilities. So when Elizabeth came in September for the community healing event, I was terribly grateful when she was willing to translate, once again, for me and Duder when *he* came a-knockin', as it were, when she was staying at my house. (He's pretty hard to say no to and, fortunately, she likes talking to him, too.) On the whole, the unplanned conversation we had confirmed for me that he was still pretty much always around or, at least, he could be around whenever I wanted him to be.

He also verified that everything I'd thought about the freeway healing in the summer was, in fact, "true." I didn't need the verification, but I loved having it. I really loved having it. (Okay, maybe I did need it.) And this was fun: when we were talking to him my grandmother and great aunts were there, as usual. What was different, though, was that they were now all buddy-buddy and he said that he looked in on them from time to time and they were all enjoying knowing one another. It was one more insight into the whole as above, so below idea, seeing that just as we meet friends and family members of people important to us, so do they over there. At least they all did.

∞

It was also during this time that I found myself saying to people who were aware of the contact I'd been enjoying with

Duder that it was as if we were actually having an extra year of our relationship, even if it was in an entirely different form. What was different, obviously, was that he was no longer in a physical body; what was the same, though, I have to admit, was the romantic connection we shared and enjoyed. The love. The partnership. In so many ways our relationship was undiminished and, in still other ways, even strengthened. It's hard to describe because I was certainly continuing on with my life, really and truly. *I am supposed to be here without him.* I wasn't pining after him and clinging to some fantasy of a physical relationship that would never come to pass. Yet it was also true that in many ways I felt as though I had an invisible partner, in the cute and amiable sense as opposed to the it's time to commit this guy and his dead partner sense. (Says me, anyway.) I did know it would not continue like this forever, but that's the way it was and it all felt healthy and appropriate.

In fact, it was an amusing phenomenon because Duder had promised me when we met that my string of two-year relationships — I'd had three of them — would definitely be broken because, of course, we were going to be together forever. In the more generally accepted manner of looking at things, we didn't quite break my streak — in fact we added to it. But in the new paradigm manner of looking beyond the confines of our bodies and this planet, the streak was definitely broken because our relationship was continuing and we were racking up another year. No doubt about it.

∞

Now I don't ever fall apart or say I can't handle something or fail to function and/or meet my obligations when the going gets tough. I'm just not that guy. Nor have I been one who excels at asking for help. Once, though, during this time of emotional roller coastering, when I was feeling particularly down and low and not at all on my game, I flat out called to Duder to ask him just be with me. *Please will you come? Just for five minutes? I need you.* Way out of character for me. It was early on a Sunday morning and I was lying in bed in such a discombobulated state and wanted so badly to feel his presence, to absorb it, to ground and soothe myself with it. And for the first time ever since he left this plane, he did not respond. Nothing. When it was clear that my desire would go unmet, I was bereft. Ten months after he had crossed over I was having a sense — for the first time — of what it felt like for him to really be gone and I wasn't liking it. It occurred to me that this must be how most people feel when they "lose a loved one."

As I have likely made clear by now, ahem, I have complete faith in the notion that *we are here for a reason* and that there are no accidents and that we are "here" in any given moment of our experience, for something. *Be present.* So Duder didn't respond for a reason and while this way of thinking — or knowing — certainly cuts down on a lot of anxiety, it can also generate some frustration because of the lag time that often emerges between the event that's for a reason and our ability to understand, if we ever do, what the reason is. It didn't feel right that my partner, my love, would forsake me like that. I mean, weren't we still connected? Weren't we still partners? Wasn't our relationship continuing on? Wasn't he paying attention? Did he not appreciate what a big deal it was for me to even ask for help? Did he not see how not responding to me only added to the emotional turmoil I was already in? Was *he* okay?

Then, somewhere during the following days, a new knowing rose to the surface of my awareness (working that claircognizance muscle). I realized that as wonderful and helpful and life-affirming and joyful and mysterious and fun and interesting as it was to have had Duder's company for all that time, as the first anniversary of his leaving was approaching, I also knew that the level of communication we were enjoying and the frequency with which we were enjoying it was not sustainable. There would be a point, soon, where instead of enhancing our individual learning and enlightenment, our high level of communication would actually inhibit it. Getting no response that day led me to knowing this and so there was the reason – or at least *a* reason – for the all-alone feeling I had experienced a few days earlier. As you know, it wasn't exactly the first glimpse I had of him as more than who I knew him to be. But I think it was truly the beginning of seeing him as something beyond my *romantic* partner which, as was becoming more and more clear, would be an essential aspect of future growth for both of us. Turns out his not showing up that morning was by design. I think they call it tough love.

As I let this knowing in, it also became obvious that the emotional hurricane I'd been living in for a while – formidable as it was – was not only about rolling over all that had happened during the previous year. I knew it! It was also very much about this extra year of partnership I'd been having with Duder and how, unconsciously, I was preparing to say goodbye to him on a distinctly different and far deeper level. The moment I hit upon that insight, it felt like the last piece of a big puzzle had been put into place. So now, at least, I was conscious – quite conscious – of the ingredients of my sappy emotional saturation: the defiant calendar and separating more from Duder.

∞

I was busy, busy, busy teaching my weekly class, coordinating the second community healing event, and wrestling with a very heavy chapter for my book. I was emotional, emotional, emotional processing through all that had happened the previous year and, now, gearing up for a super-sized goodbye to Duder. And shhh, don't tell anyone, but I was also kinda sorta thinking about maybe entertaining the notion of possibly marking the anniversary of his leaving in some way. Yes, on December 20. (He said sheepishly.) My ongoing communication with him was generally so joyful and it always felt healthy and appropriate *(listen to inspiration)* and now it was also feeling healthy and appropriate – and heartbreaking – to be thinking about separating some more (still *listening to inspiration)*. But there were miles to go before the big anniversary including honoring some annual traditions which typically keep me away from home for much of November and December.

The first is a trip in early November to the east coast for my niece's birthday. Not long after I returned from that was the second community healing event which was just as successful as the first. Done and done. After the event, three of my colleagues went home and Elizabeth stayed an extra night. We were talking about the two events, about how much people appreciated them, and then I got one of my "visions." It was for a full-on, "healing center" (though I didn't want to call it that) dedicated to raising the vibration in any and all ways known to man and woman. It had me bursting all over the place with benefits for healers, for seekers, for the town itself, and I could see five years out what a positive force for healing it could/would be. I was on fire and Elizabeth got caught up in it, too. Duder was part of it as well. I now understood why my friend had asked me about the physical place and why that woman asked me what I would call such an endeavor. But another project was just what I didn't need, so off to the back burner it went.

Thanksgiving was the next, if not original, annual tradition. I have celebrated it for about 15 straight years with very close friends who live in another state. After we'd each spent particularly hellacious Thanksgivings with our actual families one year way back when, we made the decision to celebrate from then on with our *chosen* family – ourselves. We missed it the previous year, of course, and I was looking forward to seeing them all again this time around. I treasure being with them and their three daughters (Uncle Steven!) and I draw tremendous energy from our long and close relationship. However, some things had gotten kind of funky lately – a very unusual happenstance for us. My crazy schedule notwithstanding, I had done all the coordinating of securing the house we rented, did all the food shopping, invited some agreed-to guests, no problem, the usual stuff, and suffice it to say it was about the worst Thanksgiving I ever had. I couldn't believe it had happened with them, but it did, and at the end of our five days together I was terribly hurt, dejected, and depleted. I had no doubt we'd be okay in the end, but zero energy would be going from me to them for a while. The final November-December event is that for most of the last dozen years or so, I have had the privilege of going to New York City for an extended stay at the end of the year. A friend lets me stay in her place while she heads west for the holidays and I usually coordinate my travel to coincide with hers, but I didn't yet know her plans and was so eager to get out of Dodge. The emotional whirlwind had not abated, the busy-ness was going strong, the Thanksgiving debacle almost put me under, and I was trying to find a moment to think about doing something for that anniversary I thought I didn't care so much about. So I went ahead and made my reservations and, as it turned out, I would arrive in the New York metro area about a week before my friend left for her trip.

∞

I was raring to go, but I wasn't going anywhere until I had an official reading with Elizabeth. I didn't really want to talk with Duder all that much, but I needed to ask him one question: Would he be there on December 20 if I did a thing? The truth was that I had been thinking about this thing we needed to do – this saying goodbye on another level – even though I hadn't talked with him about it or even thought about what to actually *do*. But I knew I didn't want to do it in session with Elizabeth – or anyone else – and I knew I wanted to do it on December 20. Go figure. My concern was that on that particular day, with dozens if not hundreds of people thinking about him and engaging in all manner of plans of their own, that he might be pulled in too many directions and not able to be with me. I just had to know.

And I also thought, as the contours of a something or other were forming in my mind, that my friend's apartment was the perfect place to do it because it was where Duder and I actually first got to know each other. We had met in Chicago and had eight hours together before I had to leave. The next week, we were able to grab 24 hours together in New York where he was visiting friends and I had business. That went well, very, very well, so I invited him to spend a week with me during my annual trip to New York a few weeks later – and he did. We stayed at my friend's place and as one day flowed into the next, spending 24/7 together and loving every minute of it, we kept looking at each other saying, "I still like you." The Duder thing started a week or two later when we finally spent some time in each other's environments in California.

But I digress. Bottom line, there was just no way I was going to expend any energy on this anniversary project without assurance from him that he would be there. So the day before I flew from Los Angeles to New York, into a reading with Elizabeth I went. For the last couple of months my blubbering emotionality made me feel like a saturated sponge that just leaked and dripped all over the place. Still, I kept my messes to myself and I doubt very much that anyone else really noticed. And just for the record, because I'm feeling compelled to say this, such a high level of boo-hooing or getting choked up is really not my typical m.o. So it was very unusual – even for me during this particular time – to settle into my comfy chair in Elizabeth's office and devolve instantaneously into a bumbling, crying, emotional mess. What the hell? It came on in a flash and I couldn't seem to get a grip. Elizabeth was settling in herself and when I looked at her, she was focused on Duder and looking at him, not noticing for a second that I had turned into a heap of jell-o. She was saying to him, "Oh, honey. What's wrong?" Then she told me that he was kneeling on the chair beside me and was really sad. Crying, crying, crying. Just like me. Of course. In fact, I have no doubt that's why *I* was crying so much.

And there it was again. Still. The two of us completely and utterly in the exact same place. We hadn't "officially" communicated about this whole project, this separating on another level thing, but now I knew that he knew, too, that it had to happen. And despite the sadness we were both feeling about it, it was so comforting to feel that connection again after having been so fatootzed for so long. Yes, he had been knowing what I had been knowing about our needing to separate more. Yes, it was difficult for him, too, and he even had a couple of guides who would be helping him with all of it. Very nice. And, yes, he would absolutely be there on December 20. Yes, yes, yes. He even said something about candles and music, duly noted. I didn't need or even want anything more, really, but a bit of a conversation ensued nonetheless.

I had been wondering why, on the one hand, I was experiencing a *decline* in my ability to communicate with Duder while, on the other hand, I was definitely more able to communicate with the other side and was more trusting of the whole feeling and thinking thing. He talked to me about surrendering to change and shift *(we belong to the planet, not the planet to us)* and it was another glimpse into his evolution from earthly romantic partner to non-physical spiritual partner with sage-like wisdom and advice, if you will, that was so different from our dynamic when he was here. So, so different. It was up to me to keep up with that change, he said, and to embrace it so we could continue on.

He also said he was sorry about what went down at Thanksgiving and seemed to portend that things would not be good with my friends for a while. Turned out he was right, but that's neither here nor there. He wanted me to be sure to tell them how grateful he was for how they welcomed him to their/our family in such a warm way and how much he appreciated their kids, too. Uncle Duder! (That was allowed.) Then he gave me several messages for his parents and his sister. I called my friends shortly after I arrived on the east coast to relay his messages to them. Not so much, though, with his parents and sister because I was very hesitant to offend their beliefs and sensibilities. Rock, hardplace.

And somewhere in his/our acknowledgement that we needed to separate some more, came the line "you need to have other relationships." Ugh. Or maybe it was relationship, singular, I'm not entirely sure. It came across, though, in such a sweet and kind-hearted way, and it was clear that he was offering it as an example of how other relationships would foster my growth while staying romantically connected to him, a "dead" man, might actually not. No kidding. My *belief* about having other relationships was that I'd know when it was time, it would be obvious, and it would be time when it was time, not when the calendar said so, thank you very much; none of this *you should wait a year* stuff for me because maybe it would be more, maybe even less. Though in a moderately hilarious sidebar, Duder's mother said to me somewhere between his wake and his funeral, apropos of nothing, that the girlfriend his brother had when he had crossed over waited a year before dating again. What the hell was that?! Nothing could have been farther from my mind – particularly then – but somehow I felt like I'd been cursed or, worse, *dared* not to wait a year. *Just try it.* Not that anyone had to worry about any of that. The one-year mark was almost here and I wasn't ready, not by a longshot.

Knowing that he'd be there and that we'd do something on December 20 was, again, enough for me at that point and

I was fine with ending this little confab. But he went on to say that sometime in the next year he would be going to a different place – like graduate school or something – and would have little or no contact with me, others, Earth, etc. He even made some sort of crack about how we'd always have December 20. Was he kidding me? I mean I had completely wrapped my head – and heart – around the idea that we needed to separate more and, clearly, I wasn't the only one feeling gobs of emotion about that. And I was good to do it on December 20, it felt right. But I didn't think that this other level of goodbye would mean he would be completely absent from my experience here, particularly since he told me very clearly, in that New Year's Eve discussion right after he'd crossed over, that he'd be with me for many, many, many years. So this little bombshell flew completely in the face of that and felt like way too much of a kick in the gut at the worst possible time. And excuse me but I certainly didn't want to think about a permanent commitment to doing something every single year on December 20. No offense. And I didn't want to be having this conversation. But since we were, all I wanted to know about it was when that time arrived – and I think he was saying it would be about mid-year or so – would he come to me before he went so we could say goodbye and have a full conversation via Elizabeth or something equally clear and obvious? He assured me that he could/we would and I dropped it. Enough!

Then I had a brief conversation with my spirit guide. I watched Elizabeth gaze here and there, as though she were reviewing something. Then she said he was reviewing the year that had just transpired. "Time well spent" were his exact words and that message alone was worth infinitely more than the fee I was paying for the reading. I asked him what he thought about using a pendulum (I'd learned just enough about them to be dangerous) and he said that it would certainly accelerate my learning. He also talked to me about the changes that were coming up (completing the book proposal, launching more fully into my work, etc.), and that I should not resist it because even if it felt like I might lose utter control of my life, that would not actually happen; I would still have time to myself and with my friends and all of it. He knew way more about what was coming than I did and I took his words to heart. Satisfied, we wrapped up the session with thanks to everybody and I left the next morning.

Ceremony
December 7, 2006 – December 20, 2006

I have this thing about "the holidays" – I don't like them. (Sorry.) I am perfectly happy with all of America and beyond celebrating to their hearts' contents and all I ask is that they leave me out of it. Some can do this and some, I've found, simply cannot. So I've learned over the years that I can be left out of most of it if I go somewhere other than where I live during the season. That's why I go to New York, joy to my world. It's not only a spectacular place to celebrate the holidays, but the perfect place to avoid them, too. I grew up in New Jersey less than 20 miles from the city, then lived in Manhattan for several years after college so before the beach was home and before the mountains were home, the New York metropolitan area was home – and it still is.

For the first time since 9/11, I was thrilled to be on a plane. I landed in New Jersey on December 7, a week before my friend was vacating her place, and drove a short distance to the home of some other friends. I'd invited myself to stay with them for a couple of days after which I figured I'd stay with some other friends nearby after which I figured I'd stay with my brother and his family about three hours away. And I would also be seeing more of all them during my weeks in and around New York. I was happy to be *not* at home, but I hadn't exactly struck the right chord there in New Jersey, either. I was pensive times ten and surrounded by people (our mutual love for one another notwithstanding) when I probably should have been alone. The cold, gray, damp weather was a perfect match for my mood, not in a good way. Screw it. I booked a flight to Miami and found a little studio at the beach to stay in for a few nights – just what my inner doctor ordered. I arrived there physically fatigued, emotionally and spiritually drained, and firm in the knowledge that I had some serious Duder work to do before December 20. In fact, I had been thinking about little else. There's absolutely no question that before he returned to Spirit I made peace with saying goodbye to him. Not only did I make peace with it, I said it to him directly. Several times. I said it when I had that clinical response to his questions down in Mexico; I said it in several other conversations during his last weeks at home; and I said it – without words – when he was actually breathing his last breaths. And for many weeks I'd been knowing that I was needing to say goodbye to him on this deeper level. At least that's what I thought.

What I realized on the beach was that I wasn't so much gearing up to say goodbye to *him* on a deeper level as much as I was gearing up to say goodbye to him and *me*, to *us*, to our *couplehood*. Oy. That did feel different. Given all that had transpired during the year and how connected I'd still felt to him and how I was thinking I needed to say goodbye to him on a deeper level, this was actually, somehow, news to me. But three days alone on the sand in the sun allowed me to sort it all out and I did. I left there feeling centered again and strong – just needed a little processing time, people! – and ready to mark the first anniversary of Duder's passing in grand fashion. Or in some fashion, anyway.

I arrived in the city on the 15th of the month, buoyed not only by the return of my state-of-mind, but also by a streak of extremely temperate, surely global warming-related, spring-like weather in the winter – my artful dodge of the cold, damp, gray of the week before perfectly executed. The luxury of walking around Manhattan with a middle-weight jacket and no precipitation in December augmented everything that is wonderful (for me, anyway) about New York and I was most grateful for it even if it was evidence of a planet in peril. I loved my 20 years at the beach, I was loving living in a mountain town of about 3,000 people, and I also absolutely love the pulse of the city that never sleeps. I always have. When I get back into it I'm like a kid in a candy store, caught up in the vibe and looking in a zillion different directions virtually 24/7, sleep be damned. The Chicagoan I had partnered with was one who truly loved New York, too, and with him on the brain and in the heart in a particularly huge way, it was nice to reflect, as I bounded about the city, on the three different times we shared being there together.

I was also thinking a lot about all the people from Duder's life who had loved him and were, no doubt, missing him a great deal right then. From the time he was diagnosed, he maintained email contact with them, updating everyone on his treatments, condition and progress along the way. I had my own list for the same purposes and I took over his during his last several weeks. During that time I spoke to many of them on the phone and later met some of them at his wake and funeral; some I never met. I was inspired to drop a note to all of them, to acknowledge the anniversary that was upon us, and to thank them for welcoming me, a stranger, into their hearts during a painful time. I let them know what a privilege it had been to be with Duder when he was on the receiving end of such love and compassion – a very profound aspect of the whole experience that often got lost. I also let them know I would be marking the pending anniversary "privately and with a full and open heart."

∞

There are many people in my life with whom I shared the encounters I'd been having with Duder in full. There were even more people with whom I shared little or none of it because I'm just not in the business of imposing my views or opinions or experiences on anyone who isn't interested or, more to the point, on anyone who, based on *their* beliefs, might find what I have to say to be sacrilegious or otherwise offensive. I put Duder's family in the latter category and I'm good, quite good, with respecting that boundary. Duder, however, seemed to not even see it.

As I told you, he had – in the conversation before I left California – listed a number of things he wanted me to tell his parents: that he felt their pain, too, that he loved them, that he was in a good place, and that he was learning wonderful things. Stuff like that. He wanted me to tell his sister that he loved her very much and that he and their brother – from the other side – would help her two boys be the kind of brothers that Duder and his brother were. He also wanted me to let them all know that his favorite (great) aunt, who had just crossed over in October, was fine, was giggling, in fact, was with him (for the time being, anyway), and had been warmly welcomed (much like he had been) when she crossed over. Normal stuff for him and me; blasphemy, I was thinking, for his family.

Even though I didn't expect it to happen and even though both Duder *and* his brother – a year earlier – had told me in no uncertain terms that I was under no obligation whatsoever to continue a relationship with either their parents or their sister, the fact of the matter was that in the wake of that conversation and over the course of the year, we had nonetheless established relationships of our own which I had grown to appreciate a great deal. I had learned a lot about which subjects were comfortable to discuss with them and which ones were not and it was clear to me that talking about talking to dead people was one that was not. I was, I thought, being respectful of their *beliefs* even though I would sometimes scream – on the inside – *But they're right here! They're thriving! You are not meant to suffer!* – wishing they could take it all in to ease their aching hearts.

But that wasn't my place, it never felt right to push it, and so I didn't. Why rock the boat? In any way? (This from a champion boat rocker.) It seemed so simple to me and it also seemed that my sage-like, wise, and adored partner just didn't get it. At all. He never satisfied my questions about why he was pushing this when it seemed so obvious that it could only go poorly. When I protested he gently persisted or, more accurately, ignored me, and I could only imagine that if I simply did as he asked, dispassionately, that it would serve a higher purpose that was far beyond my understanding or had nothing to do with me or both or something else altogether. In fact, I'm quite sure that was the case. Still, I figured I was doing enough good in enough other places to absolve myself of this and stay out of the messenger business. If it was that important, he could find another way – or do a better job of convincing me!

To be fair, relaying messages for him was never really a focus of any of our conversations. Much earlier in the year I made the mistake of asking him at the end of one of our encounters if he had any messages for anyone and he did; then I wussed out on delivering them because I just didn't want to violate the sensibilities of, at the time, his best friend and his sister. So I made a point to stop asking and I really can't recall how it even came up this time around. Did I ask him "by accident" or did he bring it up? Either way, here I was. Again. *Hey rock; hi, hardplace. What's up?* The last thing I wanted to do was deny a wish or desire of his and the other last thing I wanted to do was offend or push away his family. In the end, the best I was willing to muster was to use a bit of an opening with his sister. That email I had sent to "his people" prompted a bit of back-and-forth with her and I asked, flat out, what she thought I should/could do about messages from Steve he wanted to me to share. Surprisingly, she told me that she was very happy to hear anything that he had to say to her and she also agreed that I should probably not bring it up with her parents, that they were very old fashioned, and that she wouldn't say anything to them either. *Hear that, Duder?* What she *would* likely do, she said, is say something like, "Well if Steve were here, he'd probably say…" and stuff like that. I told her that since she was open to hearing about my communication with her brother(s), I'd write something to her soon.

On anniversary morning, December 20, I found a cozy little coffee shop in Greenwich Village where I parked myself for a while and reviewed the year of communication I'd had with Duder in an email to his sister, including what I'd failed to tell her much earlier in the year. I started by acknowledging the day and how fitting it was do be doing this, then I summarized what I thought were the most relevant highlights in an unedited, stream-of-consciousness manner. About two hours later, I hit "send" and, with that, extricated myself from between the rock and that very hard place. I had no idea whatsoever how it would be received, but it was my sincere hope that it would offer some sense of comfort and peace to someone who had been so profoundly challenged with grief and loss. She responded the next day with gratitude and said she had read through it once, through tears, would do so again when she had more time, and would come back with questions. That never happened – the questions, I mean. Or any conversation about it at all. *See, Duder?*

In the afternoon I went to lunch with a special friend whose husband had made his transition six weeks after Duder did. The two of them became fast friends when they began their treatments together in Mexico at the hospital's initial 28-day program. They supported one another quite lovingly during those weeks and stayed in touch afterward. And the four of us were there together in the fall when follow-up visits overlapped. They lived in New Jersey and she came into the city to meet me that day. We had so much to talk about and it was wonderful to connect with her and with Duder in yet another way. And it sure seemed like another fitting activity for the first anniversary of his departure from this plane. For his part, Duder had been hanging around me for much of the day and my concerns that he might not be able to were completely assuaged.

Evening was fast approaching, winter solstice and all, and so was the ceremony (as I was now referring to it) that Duder and I would be doing together. Earlier I had purchased some music for the occasion — something new-agey and meditative and new to both of us. I also bought a bunch of those little tea light candles and as I walked back into the apartment, I knew that the moment was upon us even if I wasn't exactly sure how it would all unfold.

∞

The first order of business was to light a fire in the fireplace of the medium-sized studio apartment. It wasn't needed to combat cold weather because it still wasn't very cold, but it sure helped with ambience. I put on the music — softly — and burned some sage to clear the air. I lit more than 30 of those little candles which I had placed all over the place — along the hearth, on the window sills, on the coffee tables, and on the bookshelves, each in its own little votive crafted by me, with love, from the finest aluminum foil. In no time a mood, a place, and an energy had been created and I was reminded of how easy it is to change the vibration in our environments and in ourselves. *Everything is energy.* I parked myself and sat cross-legged in the center of the double bed which is pretty much located in a corner of the apartment, a very comfortable vantage point. He had been around me for much of the day, but now Duder was saturating my body with waves of his energy. It was time.

I began by taking several deep, measured, steady breaths. Then I went into a light meditation of sorts, clearing my mind (not my best event), opening my heart, allowing his energy to meld with mine and reveling in our union. I made a point to align myself with the overall *intention* of this experience, which was to say goodbye to the romantic partnership we had shared for two, um, three years. And the *intention* for *that*, the biggest one anyway, was to allow each of us to grow as our souls intended. Then I remembered something from the recent conversation we'd had via Elizabeth. When Duder was kneeling next to me, both of us sad and boo-hooing, his guides supporting him, talking about what we needed to do – what we were now doing – Elizabeth's head and body went back as if she was being crowded out of where she was. Her head looked upward, eyes wide open, almost bulging, mouth open, too, with an unmistakable look of wonder and amazement in her expression. She said that Duder had just shown her what happens to his energy when we take this step – it was huge! – like Aladdin out of the bottle. It was an image that certainly underscored our *intention* of unrestrained growth. (I had to assume, danger danger, that it would be the same for me and he said it would be.) Given that I/we had been planning this for a while now, in some ways this ceremony was really about putting a period at the end of a very long sentence, to affirm something that had, more or less, already happened. More or less.

Centered and clear-intended, Duder's energy filling me and the room, I eased out of silent meditation, opened my eyes, took in the tranquil glow of the fire and the candles, and began talking to him. Out loud. Not something I had particularly planned, but it felt right. I told him that one year since he'd left, it was obvious to me that our relationship had deepened and expanded because I felt more connected to him and more in love with him than I ever had. And I did some kind of internal audio double-take when I heard myself say that and felt the truth of it in my being. I told him that I considered all of the emotion I had been feeling for the past couple of months to be a testament to our love and to the dynamism of our partnership. I also said how affirming of our relationship it was, as always, to have learned in the recent session with Elizabeth that he had been experiencing it, too. I told him how much I wanted for him to be utterly free to be all that he was meant to be, unrestrained in any way, shape, or form. I told him that letting go of *him* a year earlier was one thing but that letting go of *us* was, in many ways, actually more difficult – the second, more damning, of a one-two punch combination. I also told him that I certainly didn't see this goodbye-on-another-level as goodbye forever, and I hoped he didn't either; I said that I wanted him to "visit" me whenever he wanted to and that I wanted to be able to "call" him whenever I wanted to, all the while knowing that it would be very different. I reiterated that I fully understood how different it would be. I told him that I felt blessed to have been loved by him in his beautiful human form and how that blessing was multiplied by the experience of being loved by him absent his beautiful human form.

I was settling into the unfolding and peeked at some of what I'd jotted down in my trusty notebook while I was on the beach in Florida. I was prepared! In one section I'd listed a whole slew of specific "good times" that I had recalled from when we first met right up to when he drew his last breath. Our greatest hits according to me. There were so many distinctly separate experiences and I felt driven to pick some out and talk to him about how much they meant to me and why. I knew he knew the list, too, or could see it, or whatever, but I went on anyway, highlighting the highlights. As I did, it felt as though I was experiencing them all over again, as though *we* were experiencing them all over again. We laughed, we cried. Oh so emotional. Bittersweet. And I took note of how his presence – and my ability to feel it – didn't waver for a moment. There wasn't a shred of doubt that he was right there, fully present. Still. Not that I was surprised about it, but it certainly encouraged me to keep on talking so I did.

I imagine that most every couple has things they do that everyone does but that have special meaning for them. So, too, me and Duder. Everyone, for example, clinks glasses as they toast to this or that. When I first saw Duder, literally, I clinked his beer bottle with mine as I walked past him, marking my territory in an oh so suave and studly manner. Not stopping, I headed to the rest room with the intent to return and introduce myself. (It pretty much worked as planned.) For two solid years, clinks – of anything and everything – meant something special to us even though, of course, we could and did clink with others. Watching a sunset was another example. And there were several others, sex being an obvious one. I felt compelled to do two things about this: share from my guts what it meant to me when *we* did those things and assure him that when he saw me do them with other people – in romantic situations or otherwise – it would not be the same nor would I try to make it the same. He needed none of that, but I couldn't help myself.

Then came the PowerPoint presentation. I'm kidding, really, but my roll continued on as I moved into the *gratitude* phase of the ceremony, unfolding, as it was, as though I had no control over where it would go. *Thank you, Duder, for moving to the beach to give us a chance to be us. Thank you for understanding me in ways I was never understood in relationship with another. Thank you for the experience of a truly even, mutual partnership. Thank you for constant and joyful laughter. Thank you for all that you have done and are doing from there that enhances my experience here.* Who was I kidding? There was no way I could ever come close to thanking him for all our relationship meant to me so I told him that, too.

I moved from my position on the bed for the first time and wrote "Duder & Duder Forever" on a piece of paper. (Fourth grade, revisited.) Then, in the midst of this ceremony, I threw it rather unceremoniously into the fire and watched it burn. I was stunned when I literally felt an ache in my heart as I stared at it until it had completely disintegrated. This simple and surprisingly powerful act could have been the whole ceremony, the only thing I needed to "do." It was my in-the-moment way of acknowledging that, for obvious reasons, he was not *the* one that I'd be spending my life with and that he and I, as romantic partners – whether both here in physical bodies or, as in the last year, when one of us was and one wasn't – were over.

This led to my addressing head-on the real issue at hand: that I was still here in a body and he wasn't. And humans in bodies have desires that our non-physical friends, of course, cannot help us with. Again, he didn't need to hear this, but I did. I needed to hear myself tell him that I very much wanted the kind of soul growth that comes from day-to-day involvement with another human; I wanted the intimacy of sharing myself and all I have with another; I wanted physical contact and a flourishing sexual relationship – the basics – and precisely what he had broached with me way back in the spring and, again, slightly more forcefully, just two weeks earlier.

I rounded the whole thing out by telling him in no uncertain terms that, as a result of our partnership I would go forth into the rest of my life a bigger, better, grander version of myself – as I knew I would immediately after our telepathic sunset conversation exactly a year ago. I told him that I now embodied an expanded ability to love and to be loved and that I would bring to any future romantic experiences a panoramic and multi-dimensional view of what's possible in relationship. And as I had a couple of times throughout the evening, I stopped and asked him to communicate with me, to tell me anything at all because I was sure getting sick of the sound of my own voice. He flooded me with a big *I love you* and, with that, we brought our ceremony to a close.

∞

Even though it probably took you only a few minutes to read this little tale of our ceremony, it took me two hours to live it. Yep, a two-hour monologue. When it was over I felt pretty good. Tired, and good. Different. Relieved. And upbeat. I spoke briefly to two of my friends who had known what I was doing and then went to sleep, early, in the city that never sleeps.

Epilogue

I awoke the next morning feeling empty and sad. *What the hell?!* I figured all I could do was let those surprising feelings have their way, so I did. And twenty or thirty minutes later it dawned on me that they were because of the night before. Duh. The whole point of that two-hour anniversary special was to turn the page, to consciously separate from my romantic partnership with Duder and from him, too, on those other levels I'd been obsessing about. Well mission freakin' accomplished! Empty told me I'd cleared out some energy, Sad seemed to be missing what had been cleared out, and Higher Self was telling me time well spent; job well done; hole in heart...closing up; relationship...changing form.

I wasn't "done" with Duder, not completely. I wasn't ready to walk that day into a brand new relationship, not yet. But I knew that the lion's share of my process was behind me and that the second year of life as it was *supposed* to be, life without him as my life partner, would be very different from the first — it already was. I felt a palpable shift of energy in my body. By afternoon Empty and Sad had taken off, Possibility peeked at me from around the corner, a hint of Fresh lined my path, and a distant cousin of Excited tiptoed into a corner of the space that had opened up inside me. Something new was happening in my life and when I thought to share it with Duder, like I had shared myself with him most every day of the last three years, the thought was smothered by another more urgent one: *I don't have a partner anymore.* Hmmm. That really was one hell of a ceremony.

∞

Weeks and months unfolded and somewhere along the line I became aware that my membership in the I Lost My Spouse / Partner / Girlfriend / Boyfriend Club had been activated. Automatically. But it was a club with few, if any, kindred spirits. Most everyone I met used words and phrases like "agonizing" and "grief stricken" and "unbearable pain." A clear majority of them had been "suffering" for years and often longer, breathing a steady flow of life into the "you never get over it" chorus. I was living in a completely different universe.

As I reflected upon *my* experience (one I was, to some small degree, still having), I actually felt as though I'd been singled out of a crowd of millions, raised up, flooded with Light, blessed, anointed, and gifted with a deeper, richer, and far more layered living experience. Yes, really! I'm not saying ooh, ooh, my partner died, it was awesome, I can't *wait* to do that again. I'm saying my partner "died" and I'm here without him and I'm going to *choose* for myself what to make of that.

When I said at the outset I wasn't going to concern myself with what the psychologists or religion or conventional wisdom said, I was saying that I didn't want to buy into pre-existing *beliefs* about "grief and loss" because I didn't want to have a by-the-book "grief and loss" experience. So I eschewed…

It's a very, very painful experience for
     Pain is part of the experience;
You must go through denial, anger, bargaining, depression,
and acceptance for
     You can skip right to acceptance;
Some people die too soon for
     We return to Spirit when our soul work is complete;
Death anniversaries are really hard for
     Death anniversaries are;
Communicating with the dead is a sin for
     Communicating with the dead is healing;
You never get over it for
     You go through it

...and had a "grief and loss" experience that grew my soul and enriched my life. I didn't do it right, I simply did it according to my *beliefs*.

∞

Steve Lewis, Duder, the man who was my partner, died – never to be replicated or replaced. Yet the being part of the human being he was did not and cannot and will not ever die – it simply changed form and I know this has happened innumerable times. We, as a couple, Steven & Steve/Steve & Steve/Duder & Duder also died – never to be replicated or replaced. Yet our relationship did not and cannot and will not ever die – it simply changed form and I know this has happened innumerable times.

And in the wake of what did die, much was birthed. Like the opportunity to know Duder not just as the down-to-earth, playful, sexy, loving man I knew him to be but as a soul – journeying through lifetimes – always growing, always evolving, always becoming. And the opportunity to know myself not just as a decent guy with a perfect partner forging a new career but as a soul – journeying through lifetimes – always growing, always evolving, always becoming. And perhaps sweetest of all, this experience gave me the opportunity to know Duder and me not just as partners in life, a couple in love who loved being together, but as spiritual brothers – journeying through lifetimes – sometimes together, sometimes not, but always connected, always in some form of relationship, and always growing, always evolving, always becoming.

May we all know the joy of knowing ourselves – and one another – as more than who we appear to be.

The Middle

Gratitudes

It strikes me as a brazen miscarriage of justice – or, at the very least, a stunning misrepresentation – that mine is the only name gracing the cover of this book. For while I may be the only human who was engaged in writing it, I'm certainly not the only being who was.

So thank you, Duder, for your ongoing presence and infusions of light and love and laughs during what was a tremendously joyful writing experience. Thanks, too, for being on my team over there and for teaching me so much. I love you.

I offer heartfelt and ongoing gratitude, though it feels anemic to say it that way, to every other being of light and love on the other side of the veil who has supported and supports this work. Thanks for all you are doing to connect it with every being of light and love on this side of the veil who may be hungry for it.

∞

Bouquets of gratitude go to every one of the two dozen or more of you – friends, acquaintances, and friends of friends and acquaintances – who were kind enough to read early chapters or, later, the entire manuscript of this book. And an extra bouquet to those of you who offered very helpful edits. But mostly, I thank you all beyond words for your bountiful and magnanimous feedback which, more than you can ever know, is how the PDF's you read morphed into the book you're now holding. I know your generosity will be multiplied and returned to you directly .

(And please forgive me for not listing all your names, but I simply don't trust my ability to do so completely nor to live with the fallout of not having done so completely.)

∞

Finally, thank you to my agent, editor, and publisher. We are a great team and I look forward to meeting you all very soon. Let's do lunch.

About the Author

Steven Morrison loves living an utterly regular life in what he calls a spiritually responsible manner. He also loves helping others to do the same thing which, conveniently, is his job. He is grateful to be able to do it all – live, teach, and write – in Idyllwild, California. *An ExtraYear* is his first book.

Learn more about Steven and his work at spirituallyresponsibleliving.com or email him at steven@ anextrayear.com.

About Elizabeth

Learn more about Elizabeth and her work at elizabethaleccia.com.

About the Cover Photographs

Front: A sunset practically identical to the one described in the first chapter, from precisely the same vantage point, and very close to the same date.

Back: The author and his late partner, pre-everything, partner on left.

Made in the USA
Charleston, SC
05 February 2010